THE HARD-CORE DELINQUENT

This book is dedicated to the memory of my daughter, Mandy, who died the year the experiment was started; my wife and my daughter Jeanette.

The Hard-Core Delinquent

**An Experiment in Control and Care in a
Community Home with Education**

MICHAEL O. MAYERS

*Principal of Ardale
Community Home
with Education*

SAXON HOUSE

71067

© Michael O. Mayers 1980.

Published by
Saxon House, Teakfield Limited,
Westmead, Farnborough, Hants., England.

Printed in Great Britain by
Biddles Ltd., Guildford, Surrey

British Library Cataloguing in Publication Data

Mayers, Michael O
    The hard-core delinquent.
    1. Ardale Community Home School
    I. Title
    365.'42'0942678   HV9146.G/

ISBN   O 566 00318 X

Contents

Tables

Introduction

The main part of this book outlines one minor piece of research in just one community home with education on the premises - CH(E). It sets out to discover whether or not it was possible to really help some of the most disturbed, damaged, difficult and delinquent boys in the London area without the use of 'secure' accommodation. It was not the intention of the Ardale experiment to find a direct alternative to secure residential care for teenage delinquents: rather to seek to show that a percentage of boys deemed in need of secure accommodation may possibly be helped in an 'open' environment. Whether the findings have any significance for a reformation of the present system of residential child care or the treatment of juvenile delinquency remains open to question.

Unlike most research into sociological or criminological problems of young people, it has been carried out and recorded exclusively by residential practioners who are daily living and working with teenage delinquent boys. Many of the statistical recording methods may be far inferior to those normally used by professional sociological researchers. We were aware that there were many problems of non-detachment in working so closely with the subjects being researched and that this could influence our results no matter how carefully and scrupulously they were recorded. However, it must be stated that the 'experiment' was initially started with no intention of writing up our findings. This came much later when it began to appear that our methods were having some positive effect.

Ardale is just one CH(E). Many others may be carrying out various pieces of research of their own. The whole system of the residential care of delinquents is 'under fire' as being an expensive waste of time and public money. This is nothing new. Those of us who have been involved in the work for twenty or so years know that the mass media sheds a great deal of its concern of what to do with delinquents on to the actual practitioners. We are at the mercy of public opinion. During the approved school days, we were accused of not being too interested in 'care', but were merely agents for containment and training. The 1969 Children and Young Persons Act heralded a whole new era and concept of residential child care for delinquents. Now the pendulum is rapidly swinging back and we are accused of having no 'control' over delinquency. Because of this ever vacillating view of the role of a residential establishment for teenage delinquent boys—therapeutic or punitive—the majority of staff who work within them very rarely publish what they are trying to do. We normally allow our critics to make their frequently unfounded comments while we get on with the job of doing something about helping delinquents, well knowing that the arguments they put forward today will be the opposite of those they propound tomorrow. In this book, I have decided to go against our tradition of silence. There is so much being written about CH(E)s of a negative nature, this small piece of research may slightly help to weigh the balance.

MICHAEL OSCROFT MAYERS
Principal of Ardale CH(E)
September 1979.

viii

Acknowledgements

I wish to thank all the staff at Ardale who contributed so greatly to the Ardale experiment. Similarly, the Director and senior officers of the London Borough of Newham Social Services Department have my sincere thanks. Without their help and support, the work described in this book would not have been possible.

1 Delinquency and the delinquent in residential care

Delinquency and the delinquent in residential care

Although this book deals primarily with the 'sharp edge' of delinquency—the 'hard-core' delinquent—in one particular establishment, it is necessary to put delinquency into perspective and to take a very brief look at the history of the residential treatment of delinquents.

The background leading to the development of child care in Great Britain as known today goes back to the reign of Elizabeth I. The parish or local communities were responsible for the care of orphans, with the added help of well meaning people and religious bodies who supplemented the work being done. Orphans, young vagabonds and poor children had to work or were attached as apprentices, as laid down in the Poor Relief Statute of 1601. The Philanthropic Society came into being in 1788 for 'the protection of poor children and the offspring of convicted felons, and the reformation of children who had themselves been engaged in criminal practices'. (Saynell, 1964)

At the beginning of the nineteenth century, the child was regarded as a diminutive adult with the same punishments as adults, including imprisonment, transportation and hanging. Sir Edmund Du Cane, writing about the period, noted that of the 3,000 prisoners in London aged under twenty, over half were juveniles under seventeen. (Du Cane, 1885)

The Victorian era saw not only such pioneers of child rearing as Dickens, Carpenter, Shaftsbury and Barnardo, but many new pieces of legislation, including the Youthful Offenders Act of 1854, which gave courts the power to send children to the newly created reformatories. These new establishments were given solid backing in 1857 by the passing of the Reformatory School Act.

The Childrens Act of 1908 abolished imprisonment for children under the age of fourteen, and created the Childrens Branch of the Home Office. When this new body had inspected and 'approved' a reformatory school it was entitled to call itself a Home Office Approved School.

Boards of Guardians were abolished in 1929 and their previous functions became the responsibility of local authorities. The 1933

Childrens Act gave the courts power to commit children to the care of the local education authorities, and it was shortly after this that Ardale, around which the bulk of this book revolves, came into being in 1935 as an approved school.

Approved schools were residential establishments for the education and training of children and young people ordered to be sent to them by the courts. They were intended for children whom the courts considered to need not only removal from home but also a fairly long period of residential training, but who, if aged fifteen or over, were not so criminally sophisticated as to require training at a borstal institution.

Approved schools varied widely in origin and character. Some originated over a century previously as industrial schools for destitute children or as reformatory schools for delinquent children. The school managers were *in loco parentis* to the children; and the statutory Approved School Regulations specified certain clearly defined rules regarding the managing body, the treatment and discipline of children, and other matters designed to safeguard the welfare of those who had been deprived of their full liberty by a court order. In 1965 there were 126 approved schools in England and Wales, ninety of them being for boys. There were no co-educational approved schools.

In 1968, the Seebohm Committee published its report and recommended that a new social services department should be created which would take over the role of the childrens department. In the same year, a white paper entitled *Children in Trouble* was published. Following closely on the heels of this came the 1969 Children and Young Persons Act. When introducing this Act, the Home Secretary of the day, James Callaghan, stated that the purpose of the Act was: 'To prevent the deprived and delinquent children of today from becoming the deprived, inadequate, unstable or criminal citizens of tomorrow'.

The 1969 Act provided for the discontinuance of approved schools and their assimilation into a comprehensive residential child care service in accordance with plans prepared by twelve regional planning committees. For the first time in legal history, the 1969 Act made possible the joining together of the 'caring' function of childrens departments with the 'educational' function of approved schools. The Act has been referred to as as much an act of faith as a piece of legislation in stating that delinquents were in need of care rather than punishment and that treatment did not necessarily depend upon offences committed.

The Assistant Secretary to the Department of Health and Social Security (DHSS) issued Statutory Instruments in March 1973 regarding

2

Ardale approved school:

> This Order makes provision for the cessation as an approved
> institution of Ardale School and for the transfer of the staff
> of the school to the London Borough of Newham Council
> which is to assume responsibility after the school becomes a
> Community Home.

The majority of this book deals with one particular experiment
to help what I term the 'hard-core' delinquent. However, before
attempting to define that term, it is necessary to briefly define
what we mean by 'delinquency'. It is generally accepted that juvenile
delinquency has no single cause, manifestation or cure. Its origins
are many, and the range of behaviour it covers is equally wide. A
delinquent child's behaviour is influenced by numerous factors—
genetic, emotional, intellectual as well as his personal maturity, family,
school, peer group, neighbourhood and wider social setting. It can
never be stated too often that any generalisation about delinquency
is subject to very serious limitations. Many theories have been formulated, accepted and then rejected. In the ten years which have
elapsed since the 1969 Act, the idealistic theories of 'care' divorced
from 'control' have taken a number of steps backwards.

This is not intended to be a history of delinquency. Such theories
as Lombroso's physiological aspects of criminals, or Sheldon's definitions of delinquent youth have been researched and written about
ad infinitum. Similarly, there have been many theories attempting
to relate delinquency with intelligence. Perhaps the best argument
in this sphere is that given by D. J. West when he states:

> It is sometimes suggested that criminals of above average
> intelligence do not appear as often as they might in the
> criminal statistics because they use their intelligence to
> develop skills to evade being caught. (West, 1967)

In *Psycopathy and Delinquency* W. and J. McCord suggested that
many juvenile delinquents had a poorly developed super-ego. (McCord,
1959) Later research stated that the extroverted child was more likely
to become delinquent than the introverted child as the former is not
easily 'conditioned' and can fail to become 'adequately socialised'. In
his book *Care or Custody,* N. Tutt stated:

> The proponents of sociological theories regard delinquency
> as a social disease rather than individual deviancy. This
> approach does not exclude the physiological and psychological
> approaches since it could be argued that certain social condi-
> tions give rise to an increase in physiological abnormalities
> amongst children reared in such conditions or, alternatively,
> that the child rearing practices of certain social classes are

3

likely to increase the deviant personalities amongst those classes. (Tutt, 1974)

Many studies have been carried out using a sociological approach to define delinquency, frequently linking it with an educational approach. Sir Alec Clegg reported that children who suffer hardships and distress because of their home environment or cruel and neglectful parents frequently failed at school. (Clegg, 1968) Dr D. J. West researched the interaction between home environment and disturbances which led to delinquency. (West, 1969) Perhaps his most influential finding was that related to the social class of the families of delinquent children. According to West, the vast majority of delinquents tend to come from larger families who are financially insecure, live in poor housing and are often severely handicapped with overcrowding.

Criminal statistics provide fairly positive evidence linking delinquency with the material culture. Over 75 per cent of juvenile crime is some form of larceny. Much of this is the theft of such things as cars, motorbikes, clothing, records or cigarettes. As put by Norman Tutt:

> It can be said that delinquents have a high need for material goods but a low achievement motivation which prevents them from satisfying this need through legitimate means, therefore, they opt for the easy delinquent solution and satisfy the need through illegitimate means. (Tutt, 1974)

Over a period of years numerous delinquent boys have been asked why they got into trouble. In 1976, I met Dr William Belson, who had just published his book *Juvenile Theft: The Casual Factors* and we compared some of our findings. (Belson, 1976) Shortly afterwards, I was in conversation with C. R. Pidduck, an educational psychologist at Stamford House, one of London's largest regional assessment centres. We discussed our various independent research into juvenile theft and compared it with Belson's findings.

Pidduck had used a group of thirty boys, aged thirteen to seventeen, with average IQs, to ask two specific questions regarding delinquency:

1 Can you give me as many different reasons as possibly why you got into trouble or you think other lads get into trouble?
2 What do you think should be done to help other boys keep out of trouble?

Pidduck presented a detailed list of his findings, which much later, appeared in *The Community Home Schools Gazette*, (Volume 72, number 11, February, 1979). A year after the same two

4

questions were given to the next thirty boys coming into Ardale to see what similarity there was. As the boys were from the same area, it was felt that if the results were in any way similar it may be possible to link them up some how with Dr Belson's findings. There was very little difference in age, and only a slightly higher IQ range of the boys in the Ardale sample from that of the Stamford House research. The results are shown in Table 1.1.

Table 1.1

Results of the Ardale and Stamford House Research

	Ardale	Stamford House
	%	%
1 Need for easy money	84	80
2 Boredom	62	67
3 Parental problems	47	53
4 To be part of the peer group	45	47
5 Led on by older delinquents	33	40
6 Emulating parents or brothers	10	10
7 Unusual or odd reasons	22	27
8 No reasons given	12	9

The remarkable similarity in results, made at two different establishments with over a year's gap between them points out, probably more than anything else, why the London based youngsters who become delinquent feel they do so. Belson researched boys from London of about the same age as used by Pidduck and Ardale but the majority of them were not delinquents in the usual sense. Some of them had been before the courts, but the majority were just boys from one particular area who were paid to answer Belson's questions. His first three causal factors for juvenile theft in the London area were:

1 Permissiveness. Very few thought that it was really very serious to steal.
2 Associating with sub-cultural groups who felt that there was nothing wrong in stealing.
3 A relief from boredom and the need for excitement.

So, the three independent research projects had discovered the same similarities. The majority of delinquent boys felt that three of the specific reasons for stealing were:

1 To obtain more money because there did not appear to be any moral reason for not stealing.
2 Boredom and the need to do something 'exciting'.

3 To run with the gang and not to be seen as different from the peer group sub-culture.

As Dr Belson writes in his book: 'Whatever is done, there must be no misunderstanding about the situations: permissiveness by boys towards stealing is widespread'. (Belson, 1976)

Some of the Ardale boys reasons for delinquency

Below is a list of direct and unexpurgated quotes from some of the Ardale boys on their specific reasons. One is given from each of the eight sections shown on the previous page. Naturally, there is no indication as to which boys said what, but they are all fairly indicative of the general responses given.

1 It's alright for you grown-ups, you've got plenty of cash, but what about us. My mother gives me a pound a week when I'm home and thinks she's doing me a favour. You can't even buy two packets of fags for that. If I want some extra cash I nick it. When my old man comes in drunk, he never knows how much he's got in his pocket, so I help myself.

2 There's absolutely fuck-all to do down our way. Me and my mates get so fed up we just go and muck about. We might cause a bit of bovver but what else can you do when you live in a poxy place like I do?

3 Everytime my old woman sees my old man they start going at each other like cats and dogs. I get so fed up with it that I spend as little time as possible at home. I sometimes nick food or money to buy food just so that I don't have to go home until night time.

4 A lot of my mates have got flashy gear and all that. Most of them nick stuff from work as well as get it from social security. Your're not very likely to get a bird round our way unless you are seen in the right places with the right mates.

5 My old man's inside for nicking, but my brother is looking after the old lady. He's got a flashy Jag. now and he's never done a day's work in his life.

6 I don't see why I shouldn't do as well as my dad. He works on the docks and is always bringing stuff home.

7 I only nick from supermarkets cause my uncle has a little shop and he says the supermarkets are going to close him down soon. I think my uncle's a great bloke.

8 I dunno, do I?

Perhaps the above eight quotations from these boys should be linked with one quoted in *The Evening Standard* 4 February 1977.

The chairman of the Islington Juvenile Court, Mrs H. Halpin, when talking about the rise in crime by teenagers said:

> Obviously the community is failing because we get the kids we deserve. I think these children do these things because they are bored. They are living in a concrete jungle, their parents are fed up with them and often do not want them around. They do not, as it is commonly thought, sit glued to the television; they go out and get into mischief out of sheer boredom. Of course, some of them do it to get the material possessions which they are constantly pressured to have by the advertising in the mass media.

Turning now to the results of the second question: 'What do you think should be done to help boys keep out of trouble?' Here the Ardale results and those of Pidduck at Stamford House showed considerable discrepancies. It may have been that the year's gap between the two pieces of research was significant. The only real point of any similarity was the punitive one. Pidduck found that 78 per cent of his group felt the courts were basically too lenient. Ardale's findings on this score were 72 per cent.

The largest discrepancy of all between the two pieces of research was Pidduck's findings that 78 per cent of his group said that if more clubs, youth clubs, adventure playgrounds and sports centres were opened, more boys would keep out of trouble. Only 12 per cent of the Ardale group gave a similar answer although over 30 per cent mentioned discos as being suitable places lads might go to if they had the money to enjoy themselves and possibly keep out of trouble. Surprisingly, the discos which were supervised by a 'bouncer' who would throw out anybody who made a nuisance of himself were seen to be the most popular. Two boys boasted that they were relatives of 'bouncers' and one hoped to become one himself!

Pidduck found that 70 per cent of his group felt that social workers could do a lot more to keep boys out of trouble, but only 18 per cent of my sample said the same thing. 24 per cent said that teachers could help more by being stricter and not let 'kids muck about and dodge lessons', but it would appear that this was not so with the Stamford House group.

None of the Ardale boys felt that if courts gave them more lenient sentences it would help. Perhaps the biggest criticism of a care order came from one of my boys, one with four previous court appearances, who said:

> The courts have got it all wrong you know. I've had two conditional discharges, a three pound fine which I didn't pay anyway,

and a supervision order. Now I'm on a care order. They are too soft. If the beaks gave a few more DC orders out for a first offence, a lot of us wouldn't think we have got away with it. I mean, Sir, a conditional discharge for three robberies with two more taken into consideration. Makes you laugh, don't it?

Before moving on to the specific definitions and problems of what I refer to as the 'hard-core' delinquent, it is advisable to conclude with a few definitions of delinquency given over the past twelve months in relation to a specific question: 'How would you define delinquency?'

All I know is that there is some good in everybody. It's just more difficult to locate with some of your lads. I suppose you can blame the parents to some extent, but I'm honestly beginning to believe that some children are just born bad. You know, like some are born blind or lame.
(Local resident on recovering undamaged his car which had been stolen by two of my boys.)

Most of the problems start even before a boy is born. I know that there are numerous temptations as a child grows up, but, in my considerable experience, over ninety per cent of the problem stems from the home and family.
(Senior social worker of one of my boys.)

They get too much, expect too much, and don't have the basic discipline we had as kids. The worst thing this country did was stopping National Service. Some good honest old fashioned discipline would cut the delinquency figures in half.
(Policeman who questioned a boy following an absconding.)

I think it's all the fault of the school and the telly. I mean, teachers can't control them anymore and they do as they like. Then they come home and see things on the box we can't afford so they decide to steal. I'm at my wit's end.
(Father of one of the boys following a court appearance.)

It's all a bit of a lark really. I mean it's them or us, isn't it. There's nothing to do at nights around our place and my old lady wont give me enough cash to go out and enjoy myself.
(One of my boys.)

2   The hard-core delinquent

It must be obvious by now, that there is no clear cut definition of delinquency. Systems may change, laws may provide clearer legislation, the old may be swept aside by the new but juvenile crime, like the poor, is always with us. Officially there is no such thing as a 'hard-core' delinquent so it is necessary to define my terminology.

I have coined this phrase to cover those delinquents who, because of their behaviour attitudes, criminal patterns, overt aggression, absconding frequencies, extreme emotional problems, or need for psychiatric oversight are difficult or impossible to place in CH(E)s or who have been excluded from a number of previous residential establishments. Whatever our personal view of the 'colour problem' in Britain, it is an established fact that at least 50 per cent of boys difficult to place in a CH(E) are non-white. Many of these children have been 'tried' at a number of previous residential establishments and tend to regard themselves as 'different'. They frequently relish the idea that they are a law unto themselves because they are 'out of control' and nobody knows what to do with them.

There are numerous reasons why some delinquents are difficult to place in a CH(E), not the least of which is the phraseology of the 1969 Act which gives heads considerable choice on whether to admit or not. There are, however, four particular spheres which need elaboration—abnormal offenders, persistent absconders, highly aggressive and violent types, and anti-authority coloured children. That is not to say that a West Indian boy cannot also be a persistent absconder, or an abnormal offender has to be white. There is, more often than not, a juxtaposition of the various categories.

Abnormal offenders

'Abnormal offenders' is not a precise term, but it can be viewed as both covering those cases which have serious psychological disturbances as a major part of the genesis of the behaviour problem, and those whose primary difficulty is an organic one, including subnormality. Some form of labelling becomes necessary, although one must be aware that a fundamental weakness of certain diagnostic labels, such as 'severe personality disorder', is the implication for the development or otherwise of long term treatment programmes.

Various studies have suggested that anything between 15-40 per cent of the total sample of youngsters admitted to CH(E)s may be suffering from a serious enough degree of psychological difficulty to warrant specific treatment and to raise the probability that the abnormal condition is causally related to the offence behaviour. Two most recent and relevant studies of the incidence of psychological and psychiatric abnormality are those carried out by Dr Pamela Mason of the DHSS and Dr Masud Hoghugi of Aycliffe CH(E). In the former, Dr Mason studied 100 consecutive admissions to a boys' assessment centre and to a girls' school, as well as 141 children transferred from CH(E)s to mental hospitals. She found that the five major categories of 'mental illness, psychopathic disorder, antisocial character disorder, personality disorder, and neurotic illness' accounted for roughly 40 per cent of admissions to CH(E)s.

Dr Hoghugi, in a study of 350 random admissions to Aycliffe School in 1972, showed that 18 per cent were in need of psychiatric treatment and 19 per cent of psychiatric oversight because of the severity of the problems they presented. There is a long list of previous research carried out both inside and outside approved schools and CH(E)s, mainly unpublished, which broadly support Dr Hoghugi's findings. If abnormal offence behaviour is to be regarded as a useful criterion for singling out youngsters for special treatment, it would appear that anything between 15 and 40 per cent of current admissions are in need of special treatment.

Over many years, approved schools admitted those children who displayed the most severe behavioural difficulties and were able to offer a degree of support. CH(E)s, with a greater degree of say in whom they admit or refuse, are, in some cases, refusing to take in children with extreme behaviour problems. There is a shortage of special school places for severely maladjusted children and the same selectivity and rejection occurs. Special schools tend, in general, to reject the severely acting-out child. Again, medically run institutions tend to reject the children who do not conform with normal hospital ward patterns of care and, furthermore, have access to drug therapy as a means of patient containment or management rather than treatment. The resources of CH(E)s have never been adequate to deal successfully with this type of child, yet are constantly criticised for not doing so. It was hoped that the new youth treatment centres would provide some alleviation of the difficulties, but experience so far does not bear this out. In terms of numbers involved and the criteria for selection, youth treatment centres have failed to provide any significant relief to CH(E)s by admitting their most disturbed children.

Persistent absconders

Absconding from residential establishments has been a continual problem. However, since the 1969 Act abolished Approved School Orders, it has grown to considerable proportions. As CH(E)s still have the power to choose those children they think will respond to the treatment available, the most highly disturbed children and persistent absconders from other establishments are often unplaced. In a Home Office research study Clarke and Martin state: 'The most recent estimates suggest that about 40 per cent of the boys and about 60 per cent of the girls abscond at least once during training, and about 5 per cent of the boys and 10-12 per cent of the girls become persistent absconders. (Clarke and Martin, 1971)

For numerous reasons absconding is very undesirable, not the least of which is that absconders frequently commit further offences whilst absent. Official statistics for absconding are, unfortunately, now no longer available as they were in the approved school days. This is one of the many crosses CH(E) workers have to bear consequent to the 1969 Act. However, the heads and principals of CH(E)s in the south-east corner of England do meet frequently and absconding is sometimes discussed. Unofficial research is not optimistic. Absconding appears to have been on the increase since the early fifties and far exceeds the increase in population. In 1956 there were 6,890 admissions to boys' approved schools with a total of 2,682 abscondings. By 1970, the number of admissions had slightly increased to 7,191, but the number of abscondings had risen to 10,347. There was a similar proportionate increase in the figures for admissions and absconding at girls' schools.

Unlike CH(E)s, ordinary community homes have far less say in whom they have to admit. The problem of persistent absconding is often particularly acute. A typical example of this is a children's home in North London. This establishment tries to keep under the same roof a mixture of drug takers, children with sex problems, former Borstal detainees, former absconders from CH(E)s, highly disturbed and violent children, pregnant girls without a home, young offenders on remand from court for a few weeks, and children suddenly thrust into care and in need of a bed for the night. The absconding rate at this small (twenty beds) home has soared recently. One of the senior staff of the relevant social services department stated:

> Before the 1969 Act we certainly did not get the rate of absconding we do now. Now we get wide scale absconding from children's homes, partly because they have to take such disturbed children. Already subjected to enormous pressures,

11

the staff have to take the brunt of abscondings.

All local authorities are faced with a growing number of abscondings inherited from the former approved schools. Many of the old theories about absconding are now out dated. Although I disagree to a certain extent with some of their findings, Clarke and Martin go so far as to state that former theories about absconding usually adopted in approved schools were wrong. The underlying assumption was that absconding was a symptom or derivative of abnormality in the child, which tended to manifest itself whatever the circumstances. Steps taken by approved schools to counter absconding were, they say, ineffectual as a consequence: 'Staff in approved schools generally thought to explain a child's behaviour in terms of his personal characteristics rather than in terms of his immediate environment'. (Clarke and Martin, 1971) Using the personality theory as a basis, Clarke and Martin attempted to identify personal characteristics of absconders by comparing them with non-absconders. They studied personal variations such as age, height, weight, intelligence and numerous other factors. Their detailed findings do not necessarily concern this work, but they came to the conclusion that there was a slight increase in the number of persistent absconders. Though research indicated clearly the harmful effects of absconding, many social workers believed the practice to be good. Dr Clarke states:

> They feel it is therapeutic, an acting out of problems. Our view is that when children abscond they run away from their problems, and in doing so, they are making new problems— making matters worse. Absconding itself can be regarded as a special type of delinquent act'.

Violence and aggression

It is frequently the image the vandal or the hooligan creates which makes him so difficult to place in a CH(E). However, this category of 'hard-core' delinquent often has a very 'soft centre'. Taken away from their normal environment and peer groups, they frequently adapt quite well to a residential setting.

It is necessary to link vandalism and aggression together: for this reason, minor vandalism is divorced from the more serious kind which makes this type of child difficult to place in many CH(E)s. At Ardale we carried out a small survey of all the boys admitted between September 1977 and March 1978. Obviously not all the replies received are necessarily completely accurate, but they provide sufficient evidence of the varying categories of vandalism. The boys were asked if they had ever:

	%
Written on a wall in a public place or toilet	80
Written or scratched on a school desk	84
Smashed a bottle in a public place	68
Broken a street light deliberately	38
Smashed a window deliberately	37
Damaged a tree or plants	72
Damaged a bus or train seat	22
Let off a fire extinguisher in school	8
Stated never to have done any vandalism	4

When looked at like this, the results are frightening, and there are serious reservations about the 4 per cent 'innocents'. However, many of the above categories are 'minor vandalism', i.e. knocking the heads off a few flowers. In his book Stan Cohen would refer to the above as 'secondary vandalism' which follows what he refers to as 'play vandalism' in which young children damage things by accident—trees they are climbing, or scribbling with chalk on pavements for games, such as hop-scotch. (Cohen, 1973)

As children get older, many cease to commit any acts of positive vandalism, but a few continue and this usually becomes a group phenomenon—e.g. seeing who can break the most windows in a row of empty houses. The most serious form of vandalism, and the one which tends to put a child into my 'hard-core' category, is that which Cohen refers to as 'instrumental vandalism'. Here the damage is less for enjoyment, but more as a means to some other end. Included here are acts of damage where the object is to steal, as in damaging telephone kiosk coin boxes; stripping lead from buildings; destroying chairs and cupboards while committing burglary, and so on. Other examples are the destruction of certain records to cover up some illegal activity; to revenge oneself upon somebody by destroying what they cherish, a new car, a garden lawn, or smashing up and soiling a house; or to further political aims or sabotage. This kind of vandalism accounts for a minor part of young people's delinquency, and it is just this small group of 'heavy vandals' that I refer to as 'hard-core' in this context.

In fairly recent sociological research in American juvenile delinquents, the school is characterised as one of the major instruments in the increase of violence. Cloward and Ohlin suggest that lower class delinquents suffer from unequal access to educational facilities. (Cloward and Ohlin, 1955) A. K. Cohen (Cohen, 1955), points to their failure in the classroom, and Miller and Kvaraceus argue that a conflict of culture between school administration and lower class students is precipitating delinquent behaviour. (Miller and Kvaraceus, 1959). British schools are not yet quite as 'violent' as their American counterparts, but we are all aware of the rapid increase in violence to some staff in some comprehensive schools. A very large percentage of the 'hard-core' groups admitted to Ardale, had been involved in some violence to staff in their previous schools. Below is an extract, completely unedited, from a tape recorded talk I had with one of the first boys admitted in the experiment to take in boys no other CH(E)s would consider. The boy concerned, whom naturally has been given a false name, had been in Ardale for four months when we had this conversation. There was nobody else present and the boy soon forgot the tape recorder was running.

'You've been here four months now. Did you think when you arrived you would stay in any school so long?'

'No way, man.'

'Why?'

'All the schools I'd been to were shit and I didn't see why this one would be any different.'

'You were kicked out of your last school for hitting a teacher.'

'Hold on, Sir, that cunt hit me first. I bet it never said that in the report from the school.'

'Come off it, Pete. You know damn well that if you tried to hit me, I wouldn't just sit here and let you.'

'That's different. I know I'd deserve it. It was different with old ...... He was a right prick with the lads. He kept on and on at me for coming in late and I told him I'd got a good reason because my mother was ill and I'd been to get her some medical stuff.'

'Now who's kidding who, Pete?'

'Well it wasn't true. I'd just overlaid, but I wasn't going to tell that prick, was I. He should have believed me.'

'I wouldn't.'

'No but you would have listened to me and not pissed me about. You'd have done something like stopping my weekend leave and then that would have been it. Old ... just kept on nagging and nagging so I told him to go fuck himself.'

'Then what happened?'

'You know, Sir, it must be in my reports.'

14

'They only tell me what they said you did. How about letting me hear your version?'

'Well I reckon we were both a bit steamed up, and when I told him to get fucked he just blew his top and cuffed me round the ear-hole. All I did was to swing back at him and knocked his glasses off.'

'The report says you knocked him to the floor and kicked him.'

'I don't know, perhaps he only fell. I don't think I put the boot in, but I trod on him as I ran out of the room.'

'He was in hospital for two days you know.'

'Look, man, it was his own fucking fault. If he hadn't kept on nagging me, he wouldn't have got hurt and I wouldn't have got nicked the same day. Does it say in the report that one of the Old Bill punched me in the guts... I bet it don't ...'

The actual report of the above incident, including independent statements from every child in the class, states quite clearly that the teacher did not strike the boy. It appears that he was so frightened he tried to push past the boy to get out of the room and seek assistance. He has since resigned and given up teaching completely.

It is worth noting a few typical points from the above conversation. Note the bravado use of the word 'man' at the beginning, which quickly changes to 'Sir' as the boy begins to feel relaxed, but reverts again towards the latter part of the conversation. To tell a lie is quite in order, but it is also necessary to be very indignant when it is not believed. At no time is any remorse visible or evident, even though the incident was very serious. Note the final 'clincher' which states that it is quite in order to thump and kick a defenceless teacher, but the police (Old Bill) should never be rough. This is fairly typical of the violent outbursts which place many Ardale boys in the 'hard-core' category.

Anti-authoritarian coloured boys

This is quite an emotive discussion point as almost half the boys involved in the 'Ardale Experiment' have been black, brown or half-caste. Like all delinquents, they regard the police as racially prejudiced. This is a typical comment from a coloured boy at Ardale when asked about the police:

The Old Bill always pick on us, harassing us because we're

15

black. You wouldn't like it if a fucking copper came up to you and started frisking you if you hadn't done fuck all. Every time me and my mates stand outside a shop or in a bus queue, the Old Bill are down on us and run us in for 'sus' just because we're black.

Most delinquents come from deprived areas and, quite predictably, the most deprived section of the community (i.e. black youth) are over-represented. Second generation West Indian children have been forced by circumstances to grow up the hard way. The majority have learned that educational equality is no more than a political myth. Most of them have experienced the worst conditions of discrimination, overcrowding, and deplorable housing.

They have grown up where racism has become more than a mere political issue and, in many areas, where the relationship between the police and black communities has considerably deteriorated. In *New Society,* 23 September, 1976, Alan Marsh describes research he carried out to indicate racial feeling, using the Social Science Research Council Survey Unit as a scale. The basic findings were that 12 per cent of the white population were completely hostile to the blacks and 30 per cent were fairly hostile to all coloured immigrants. According to Marsh, since the 1960s, there has been a definite negative drift in British race attitudes.

In attempting to decipher the causes of 'hard-core' delinquency with the coloured population of this country one quickly finds an explosive social condition which appears to have relegated the blacks to the edge of society. For many West Indian school leavers the only real future they can look forward to is unemployment. It is out of such boredom that street crime and delinquency emerges.

During the past decade, considerable literature has been produced which discusses all aspects of the racial question, including delinquency. Some theorists conclude that the problem is a cultural one, others a sociological one. Many appear to feel that the police have over-reacted to black delinquents, and use the power of 'sus' indescriminately—i.e. the police have the power to arrest a person 'on suspicion of intending to commit a crime'. It is not the intention of this book to seriously contribute to or for these arguments although Ardale's dealings with the police indicate that, in the main, they treat all delinquents as individuals irrespective of their colour. However, stereotypes have been formed and the majority of black delinquents entering a CH(E) seem to use a similar argument to the one given by one of my 'hard-core' boys in 1976: 'What the hell does it matter? Whether we have done anything or not, we are all alike to the law. They think we're all fucking gorillas.'

What is often forgotten is that a number of white youths are also arrested on 'sus', but it is frequently those who are known delinquents or come from a known criminal family. In March 1977, I decided to check with every boy in Ardale (black and white) their experience of being arrested as a suspicious person. At that time there were eighty-five boys in Ardale, forty-one of them coloured (two Asian and thirty-nine negroid or half-caste). I asked two questions:

	White	Coloured
1 Have you ever been arrested for 'sus'?	Yes 11	Yes 27
2 Were you arrested for 'sus' before you had a record or were known to the police?	Yes 0	Yes 15

The results are significant—eleven out of forty-four boys who were non-coloured (25 per cent) had been arrested for 'sus', but none of them had so far been taken into custody prior to being known by the police either as individuals or members of a known delinquent family. Of the eleven, eight of them had been arrested while they were absconders from Ardale, and six of them admitted to me that they were intending to commit a crime when they were apprehended. However, twenty-seven out of forty-one (67 per cent) of the coloured boys had been arrested on 'sus', and fifteen of them (37 per cent) had been arrested before they were known to the police or had a criminal record. It would appear from these statistics that, in certain areas of London, the police are more suspicious of groups of coloured boys than they are of white boys.

It must be obvious that although the problems and delinquency of the negroid boy are discussed, little reference is made to the Asian child. There are very few Asian boys in CH(E)s when compared with other ethnic groups. The solidarity of the average Asian family group and community may have much influence on these findings. During the 'hard-core' experiment, there was never one single Asiatic boy in Ardale who could be categorised in this way.

Whatever criteria is used, it is increasingly obvious that delinquency amongst young West Indians is causing serious concern, although it is only a comparatively small proportion who offend. The majority of their parents are notable for their overwhelming respect for law and the forces of order.

In this brief outline of delinquency by coloured boys, emotive phrases and words such as 'mugging' are not used. However, crime involving violence to the person amongst coloured delinquents is taking a sharp rise. Each year the metropolitan statistics show a definite increase. Yet, 'violence' in this context is difficult to define because of the emotive aspect of black crime. An old lady jostled at a bus stop or in a shop queue may complain that she was

17

'attacked'. A young white woman who is accidently bumped into may say a coloured youth has attempted to sexually assault her. Some old ladies are attacked by black youth and some white women are raped or sexually assaulted, but this is far less than the mass media would have us believe. It is this image, which labels the average black delinquent as being far more difficult to handle in a CH(E) than his white counterpart. Experience shows that this is not necessarily so. Black or white, all boys are individuals and if treated as such, with a fine balance between care and control, they will react as individuals. This does not mean that the coloured delinquent is not a problem but, in the main, he is no greater or lesser problem than the white delinquent.

The delinquent who is difficult to place in a CH(E)

This chapter has attempted to take a general look at some aspects of delinquency, concentrating on the four main categories which appear to make a boy difficult to place in a CH(E). Pressure for places at the regional assessment centres make it obvious that a boy assessed for a CH(E) has to be placed somewhere, even if it is initially back home with all the problems and possibilities for further delinquency this usually entails. There has always been a certain degree of concern for the wrongly placed child, for not even regional assessment centres are infallible. In 1973, 48 per cent of the boys assessed at Stamford House were deemed as being in need of a CH(E) placement but had to be sent home because either no place was available or no CH(E) was prepared to accept them.

The 1969 Act has many critics. It has been praised and it has been cursed. It has a number of excellent points as well as a considerable number of faults. However, it has one extreme 'loophole' which was never envisaged: it allows heads of CH(E)s to admit or refuse a boy with virtually no reference to any other person or body. In theory, heads should consult with a representative from their social service department chosen by the director, but as these people usually rely heavily on the advice of their CH(E) heads it is frequently a mere formality to seek approval for refusing a boy. It would be a very brave and perhaps foolish local government officer who insisted that a head should take a boy he felt he could not help. The majority of CH(E) heads have used this 'power' of refusal with considerable discretion, but there would appear to be some evidence that, on occasions, it has been abused.

18

3   The Ardale 'hard-core' experiment

A general description of Ardale CH(E)

Ardale, which was originally an orphanage run as the Stepney Boys' Home at the early part of the century, has seen many changes. In the early 1930s it became a reformatory school and, upon obtaining official approval from the Home Office became an approved school in 1935. Although the LCC, and later the GLC, initially administered Ardale, this passed to Essex in the 1950s.

Ardale, along with one other similar establishment in Cambridge-shire, earned the reputation of being regarded as an approved 'grammar' school, catering only for delinquent boys with superior and above average intelligence. This situation continued until the implementation of the 1969 Act when Ardale became a CH(E) administered by the London Borough of Newham.

It is situated half way between London and Southend, just off the main A13 trunk road, in North Stifford, a small Essex village. It derives its name from the Ardalles, the sixteenth century Lords of the Manor of North Styfford. Ardale stands in thirty-seven acres of its own grounds and some of the original buildings still exist, including the very impressive water tower which is a local landmark and the first view any traveller by road gets of the establishment. The four house units and the education centre are purpose built and stand separate from each other. In addition to the main buildings, offices and staff accommodation, Ardale has its own heated indoor swimming pool, tennis court, gymnasium and sports fields.

Although considerable staffing changes have been made (see later chapters), during the entire course of the Ardale experiment, the staffing consisted of a principal, two deputy principals, senior teacher, matron, assistant matron, four house wardens, eight house-masters, four housemothers, one social caseworker, nine teachers and/or instructors, four night supervisors, three administrative and clerical staff, five maintenance and grounds staff, and approximately twenty-five domestic staff. The school had, and still has in 1979, the services of a visiting consultant psychiatrist, medical officer and chaplain.

One of the consequences of the Ardale experiment was that it highlighted the need for a considerable increase in basic residential child care staff and a reduction in the number of boys on roll. During the experiment, Ardale catered for up to 100 boys, twenty-five in each house unit. The three main criteria for admission (between 1973 and 1978) were that boys should be between thirteen and seventeen years of age, come from one of the London boroughs (except in a small percentage of 'special' cases), and be of 'average to above average' intelligence. The actual number of boys was increased from less than forty in 1973 to more than ninety by 1976.

The aims of Ardale CH(E)

In 1973, it was decided to formulate a brochure about Ardale which would be useful to social workers, parents, visitors and new staff. This has been considerably updated recently and individual brochures are available for the various groups. In both the original and updated brochures, it was felt necessary to clearly state the aims of Ardale, which are:

1 To provide a programme of care, treatment, control and education for a group of boys who may be disturbed, deprived, or delinquent, with the object of building up their self-image, increasing their self-discipline, and enabling them to make a better adjustment to present day society.
2 To provide each boy with a feeling of security in a caring situation, where genuine relationships can be fostered.
3 By various methods, including individual counselling, group therapy and behaviour modification, to help each boy adjust better into society when he leaves Ardale.
4 To provide each boy with an individual treatment programme, based on *genuine* needs and to see that all recommendations and suggestions are implemented.
5 To provide four completely different house units, each capable of dealing with a number of specific problems, and staffed accordingly with qualified and experienced staff.
6 To work closely with social workers, local authorities, parents, outside agencies and interested parties to the best advantage of each individual boy.
7 To offer academic education from a remedial level to external examination level, depending upon each boy and his individual circumstances.
8 To provide a series of *realistic* vocational training schemes to help each boy when he leaves, irrespective of whether or not he

eventually intends to take up as permanent employment any trade taught to him.

9 To encourage students, research workers, community service volunteers, and other interested parties to take part in the corporate life of Ardale.

10 To encourage all untrained staff to obtain the necessary experience and qualifications to enable them to function more adequately in their professional roles.

The reasons for formulating the experiment

In the days of the approved schools, heads received their children through a general classifying and pooling system so that, as far as possible, the right child went to the right establishment. Even in those days there were a number of very difficult children, but these were 'pooled' so that no one particular approved school had more than its quota. The 1969 Act changed all than.

The period of uncertainty and change over between 1969 and 1973 was a difficult one. CH(E)s were seen as approved schools with another name and were regarded by many social workers as 'the final solution' if everything else had failed, but never to be used as a first preference in child care. Consequently, for a lengthy period, most of the children offered to CH(E)s were the failures of other systems, particularly the failures of other residential homes. It is not really surprising that a few CH(E) heads began to refuse almost as many children as they accepted.

The situation almost reached a public scandal. Magistrates were appearing in press reports maintaining that they were putting children on care orders one day and seeing them in the same courts again the following week. Social workers were complaining that they had tried CH(E) after CH(E) but they all had some 'legitimate reason' for not accepting or, if they did accept, only offering a place three or six months hence. Residential staff were concerned at the bad publicity they were getting, often not even realising that their own head's policies were considerable contributing factors. The police were 'up in arms', taking the main attack to the social workers with whom few could communicate. The regional assessment centres were becoming clogged with children they could not place. Directors of social service departments were so immersed in re-organisation that they just accepted it as a minor irritant amongst a legion of irritants. And, the mass media had a field day.

The situation in the regional assessment centres reached such a crisis that the principals of two of London's largest were forced to issue an edict restricting length of stay after assessment to three weeks.

At this stage, in the autumn of 1974, I formulated the idea of admitting a few of the 'difficult to place' boys on a 'succeed in two months or leave' basis. My fundamental thinking at that time was extremely unsound, nor, looking back in retrospect, was it very good child care. It did, however, allow a slight release of the constriction at the RACs which primarily dealt with London delinquents.

On the two month trial basis, Ardale admitted two boys and, to the surprise of myself and all my staff, they fitted into Ardale at least as well as the boys admitted 'normally'. However, Ardale may have merely taken a couple of boys who had been wrongly assessed or who had been pushed from pillar to post so often they were themselves relieved to be finally offered a place.

The initial steps of the experiments

The two boys admitted in 1974 had been at Ardale for over a fortnight before I finally made up my mind to give serious thought to taking more. I dug out the papers on the boys previously refused and sought information from the RACs on boys who had been refused admission at other CH(E)s. Eventually, it was possible to draw up a list which showed that every boy refused admission had a combination of the following characteristics:

1 Anti-social attitudes, particularly towards adults.
2 Overt aggression to peers.
3 Criminal sexual problems.
4 In need of psychiatric oversight or attention.
5 Extreme emotional and/or behavioural problems.
6 A history of truanting or absconding.
7 Had been excluded from a school or other residential establishment.
8 Was non-white.

The first three were 'normal' characteristics of many delinquent children. Look at the old files of any approved school from 1940-69 and you will find these problems. Psychiatric problems did not necessarily mean that the boy was a raving psychotic. What child in care does not have some form of emotional or behavioural problem? Six and seven are both normal 'characteristics' of any CH(E). The final one was worrying, and I had to carefully check through my figures and statistics to see if I had not made a mistake. The facts, however, stood out quite clearly—boys were frequently being refused admission to some CH(E)s because they were big, aggressive and black. To the best of my knowledge, this fact was rarely, if ever, referred to by the Commission for Racial Equality, or the Race Relations Board as it was then known, even if they were aware of it.

Knowing that it would not be long before people were asking why Ardale was prepared to admit the most difficult type of boy, it was felt advisable to draw up a list of the pros and cons and I quickly found that the few advantages were outweighed by the considerable disadvantages:

Possible advantages

1 To help relieve the pressure of the Regional Assessment Centres.
2 To assist social workers in placing boys who seem to have no alternative but to be returned to their home environment and delinquent sub-culture peer group.
3 To give a breathing space for parents and families.
4 To know that the experiment with each boy could be terminated if necessary by a pre-arranged written assurance before the boy was initially admitted.
5 As a means of carrying out specific research which could, in the long run, be beneficial to practitioners of residential child care.

Possible disadvantages

1 Would two months be long enough to be able to evaluate whether or not the placement could be made permanent?
2 How would a boy react to knowing he was at Ardale on trial? Should he be told and, if not, what would be the consequences if he found out by accident?
3 With those boys who failed and left after two months—for it was obvious that we must have our failures—would it not further reinforce a boy's feeling of rejection by society?
4 What would be the attitude of social workers and parents of other boys who absconded because of pressure put on them by the two month trial boys?
5 In this era of 'nothing succeeds like success', what would be the attitude of Ardale's managing body if the success rate (whatever that is) dropped because of this specific group?
6 How would the remainder of the boys react and would the general atmosphere at Ardale drastically change?
7 Would the Regional Assessment Centres think of Ardale as taking any and every boy offered, thus creating a dustbin syndrome?

Would it eventually get to the stage where they were saying that Ardale only catered for the very difficult child and 'normal' delinquents were not accepted?

8 Would other CH(E)s regard the Ardale experiment as stupid, foolish, brave, daring, ambitious or just plain sensation hunting?

9 What decision could be made for the boy who seemed to be making personal progress while at the same time disrupting life for other boys and staff?

10 Could the staff cope with the extra problems for no obvious rewards?

11 Would the violence within Ardale escalate to such proportions it became either unmanageable or reached the mass media?

12 Would Ardale lose some staff specifically because of the experiment?

13 What would be the attitudes of boys, staff and managers to what would probably amount to a considerable increase in the non-white population of Ardale?

14 Would the present black minority become the power group at Ardale and would we be able to control it. Would we be creating a hydra?

15 Could the managers and director be convinced in advance that this was a viable experiment?

16 Were our motives really honest or were we merely experimenting for the sake of experimenting, with the possible intention of writing up any findings for possible publication?

17 Did I really want to accept all the enormous problems of the experiment and research?

18 If the experiment was going to be a genuine piece of child care research, should comparison groups be used within Ardale and possibly even at another CH(E)?

19 Would the tiny number of 'hard-core' boys likely to be admitted to Ardale make any real difference or significance to the problem on a national or international scale?

20 What would happen if the experiment was a total disaster? Was it worth taking the probable risks for what was, after all, a leap into the dark?

The advantages and disadvantages of such a scheme were considerably weighed up while, at the same time, the initial two boys were very closely observed. A decision had to be made and, finally, the only logical one was arrived at. The main function of a CH(E) is to help deprived and delinquent children go through one of the most difficult periods of their lives. Slowly, but with ever increasing momentum, the Ardale experiment began to take shape.

Questions and hypotheses

In autumn 1974, when the scheme began, I knew that if anything was going to be proved or disproved about residential child care practices, we would have to be strictly honest with our methodology and would have to keep painstaking records, not only of the experimental group but any comparison groups used. I coined the phrase 'hard-core' delinquents at about the same time but really wondered if there was any such being. It was felt that we would have to evolve some fairly definite criteria for success and failure, and that very little could be proved or disproved until well over half the boys in the experiment had left Ardale for at least twelve months and possibly longer. Finally, the following eight hypotheses were formulated which were intended to be used as a yardstick when evaluating the scheme:

1 The experiment should show distinct alterations in the educational, behavioural and social patterns of the boys concerned as compared with their previous case histories prior to admission to Ardale.
2 This pattern should, at least, compare favourably with the various comparison groups used.
3 There should be a distinct change in the general life at Ardale. This experiment should show whether this is, or is not, a good thing.
4 It should show whether or not the staff of a CH(E) are capable of dealing with 'hard-core' delinquents. If not, it should indicate how the scheme could be improved.
5 It should hopefully show a marked pattern of improvements, in relation to previous criminal history, of the boys involved in the experiment after they have left Ardale, provided they leave in normal circumstances.
6 It should show that the coloured delinquent is, in the main, no more difficult to help than his white counterpart.
7 It should indicate certain areas in which boys classed as 'hard-core' delinquents have similarities and dissimilarities for future researchers to study in more detail.
8 In view of the present outcry over the expensive use of CH(E)s, it should give some indication as to whether or not there is any value in continuing this expensive form of residential treatment.
It should also indicate if there is need for the creation of special secure CH(E)s to deal primarily with the 'hard-core' delinquent, should all the findings indicate that he cannot be helped in an open CH(E).

The secondary stages of the experiment

This really consisted of three sub-stages as follows:

1 Getting the support of the staff.
2 Setting up various comparison groups.
3 Devising tests, questionnaires, and the methods for obtaining specific results.

Getting the support of staff

Despite any doubts which existed, most of Ardale's staff quickly became involved in the experiment to various degrees. To counter the expected apprehension, the main argument used was that there was very little to lose as the experiment could very speedily be terminated if absolutely necessary. It must be stated that, to some extent, a need to know process was put into operation and a good percentage of the staff were only concerned at the periphery of the experiment.

Ardale had, as previously mentioned, four house units, each capable of admitting up to twenty-five boys. It appeared obvious that one of them should be especially geared up to take the 'hard-core' group as they were admitted. One of the house wardens and his wife—the housemother—were asked if they would be prepared to take on the heavy responsibility of admitting some of the most difficult boys in the country. They were well aware that there were no financial perks attached to this, but their previous work had indicated that they were very caring and consistent people who both loved a challenge.

Once they agreed to accept the challenge, we gradually ran down the numbers in the house, brought their junior house staff into the discussions, and spent a lot of time and some considerable cash in letting the remainder of the boys in the house paint, decorate and partly refurnish. Meetings were held with the nucleus of lads remaining in the house and, although they were not told an experiment to help very difficult boys was being planned, they were informed that their house was becoming a special admissions house, and that their role would be to help the new boys to settle in. There was no intention of starting a prefect or big brother system, but experience had shown that new boys settle into a house much quicker if the boys already present are reasonably happy and contented. This, in retrospect, was probably one of our wisest decisions.

After twelve months of the scheme, I was asked by the Director (now retired) to prepare full facts and figures of the scheme which he accepted. A partial summary of these facts and figures was later published in *The Community Home Schools Gazette*, October, 1975, but this was a full year after the experiment had started.

Setting up comparison groups

Initially it was intended to run one or two comparison groups at other CH(E)s. It would have been possible to elicit the support and co-operation of a number of heads, but I well knew that the time and extra effort needed for this would be so vast that the work at Ardale would naturally suffer. I thought of asking a few of my friends at other CH(E)s to administer certain tests for me, but in the end decided to keep the experiment completely within Ardale. Perhaps the insularity of our findings makes some of them suspect, but this will not be known until other establishments carry out similar schemes.

Within Ardale, from the beginning, it was decided that if the experiment was to reveal anything at all, it could only do so by direct comparison with other boys in the school. Two specific groups were used. The first was a pairing group. This simply meant that when boy A was admitted into the 'hard-core' group, the next boy admitted normally became boy B and was used as a direct comparison with boy A. As both groups increased, the various and varying group pressures and norms made this difficult to operate. The second group was spread throughout the two year experiment and consisted of a completely random sample of twenty-five boys taken from the normally admitted boys.

Nobody but my two deputies and the housewarden of the 'hard-core' house were aware that we were running comparison groups. As we administered a number of tests to far more boys than we actually recorded for comparison purposes, very few staff and no boys were aware that we were continually cross-referencing the 'hard-core' boys.

Devising tests, questionnaires, and general methodology

As the various tests and questionnaires used are described in detail as and when they arise, they are but briefly mentioned here. Suffice it to say, at this stage, that much thought was given to choosing and devising tests which would be able to prove or disprove the various hypotheses. One of the first tasks was to devise criteria for success and failure. The old Home Office definition was almost exclusively linked with reconviction after leaving an approved school. Although there are no statistics, it is likely that there were many ex-approved school boys who have been deemed a success by the Home Office criteria merely because they have not been caught committing

27

further offences during the twelve month period. Obviously in any research involving follow-up when boys have left an establishment such as Ardale, a history of further court appearances has to be considered when trying to judge success and failure, but this was too narrow to be the only criterion, so it was thought appropriate to divide the success ratings into two areas: within Ardale, and after leaving Ardale CH(E).

Establishing criteria for success within Ardale

1 To complete the initial trial period and be accepted into the school following a case review, as with the normal entrants.
2 To be allowed to be officially absent for holiday and leave periods and to regularly return on time without having got into any further trouble with the police.
3 To successfully complete a length of stay at Ardale, mutually agreed by the school, the social worker and general circumstances. And, to leave with a firm prospect of employment or a return to normal state education.
4 To considerably lower aggressive and/or absconding patterns, although a certain degree of both would be accepted in the initial stages.
5 To avoid any court appearance which will terminate the experiment: i.e. being sent to a detention centre or Borstal.* This did not mean that a boy from the experimental group who made a court appearance and was awarded a non-custodial sentence such as a fine, was deemed to be a failure.

Establishing criteria for success after leaving Ardale

1 To obtain and keep employment for at least a year[†] after leaving Ardale. This did not preclude a boy from changing employment, but not too frequently and for valid reasons only. Or, to return to a state school and attend regularly without persistent truantism.
2 To not receive from any court, for at least one year after leaving Ardale, any custodial sentence. Or, not to appear in court

---

*As the experiment proceeded, there were occasions when a boy was sent to a detention centre but was re-admitted following completion of his sentence. In these cases, as illustrated later, this was not regarded as permanent failure.
†Initially, we worked on a basis of six months so that we could get some feed back. As time progressed, this was extended to one year.

more than once (except for remands or adjournments) on any charge, whether or not the sentence was custodial or otherwise.
3 From follow-up research, compared with similar research for the other groups, to prove that the 'hard-core' group are making genuine efforts to conform to other sociological norms of society, viz:

Parental relationships
Peer group/sub-cultural relationships
Emotional and/or normal sexual relationships
Membership of youth clubs or similar organisations
Marriage and/or fatherhood.

Details of the groups used

Including the two boys admitted before starting the experiment proper, we decided to work on an initial two year basis—August 1974 to August 1976, and to follow-up the school leavers for at least one more year.

Group A

Fifty boys defined by our terminology as 'hard-core' delinquents. All were boys from the various London boroughs, all were on full care orders, and most had been refused a place at at least one other CH(E) for one reason or another.

Group B

Twenty boys in Ardale admitted at approximately the same time as the first twenty 'hard-core' boys by the normal processes.

Group C

Twenty-five boys admitted normally, selected at random during the main part of the Ardale experiment.

Staff groupings

The quality of life for boys or girls in a CH(E) is, to a very considerable extent, determined by the attitudes of the staff towards their work. Residential social work is very difficult, both intellectually and practically. By the very nature of their work, staff are daily exposed

29

to quite severe emotional strain in trying to help the children in their care. They can be very vulnerable and need to be able to share concerns and anxieties in an atmosphere of confidence and trust.

It is essential that they are aware of the general policies of their establishment. It is for this reason that I have prepared and issued to all my staff on appointment a brochure entitled *A Guidance for all New Staff at Ardale* in addition to our *Policy Brochure*. Being fully aware of the problems the experiment could cause to the staff, it was necessary to convince them that many boys labelled as unhelpable were in greater need of help than any other boy in the school.

There are two words which sum up work in CH(E)s. They are care and control. Without some form of control there can be no real care. Without care, control becomes automatic and often brutal. In the early 1970s, control became a dirty word and few CH(E)s became therapeutic, allowing the children an over abundance of free choice and decision making. Some of these worked well—for a time at least—but the later 1970s saw a more realistic return to the idea that certain decisions and rules must be made and kept.

Setting up a house for the 'hard-core' group

It was obvious from the start, that it would be necessary to completely alter the ethos in one particular house unit and that I would need the whole-hearted support of the senior staff in that house. I have briefly mentioned my initial approach to the housewarden and housemother of Shackleton House, the one chosen to become the 'hard-core' unit. One of the biggest disadvantages in 1974 was the difficulty in giving extra staff to this one house. One of the hidden advantages of the experiment was to highlight the urgent need for an increase in child care staff at Ardale. The initial problems within the house appeared to be:

1 To convince all staff concerned of the need to deal with a tougher type of boy. This meant basic discussions on linking control with care in a manner not carried out before at Ardale.
2 The transfer of at least one extra member of staff from one of the other three houses, and persuading the staff in these houses that one house was not going to get all the perks.
3 The numerical run down of the boys in the house so that only a small nucleus of reliable boys would be left to form the basis of the new groupings.
4 The need to decorate and partly refurnish the house in order

30

that, even materially, it would be seen to be different from the other three.

5 To plan in detail how the treatment would be different, from the time of admission to the time of release.

6 To involve other staff—educational, psychiatric, counselling, volunteer, etc., in the new system of treatment programmes, behaviour modification, etc.

In 1974, the normal house set up was one housewarden, one housemaster and one housemother for twenty-five boys. To this was added two teachers who independently worked from 6.00 to 10.00 p.m. on two evenings per week and who shared the work with the housestaff on one weekend out of three. There were also two other housemasters, one of whom was usually on a full time qualifying course and therefore out of Ardale. The other acted as relief housemaster, covering each house in turn as staff went on leave or were absent for any other reason. Looking back, with the poor ratio of boys to staff, it is difficult to imagine how we even managed to control, never mind care for the lads. Half way through 1975, I was given an increase of two more housemasters.

The housestaff worked on a day on duty/day off duty basis during the five day week, and worked two out of three weekends. Sheer necessity made it essential to close every house unit from 2.00 p.m. to 5.00 p.m. This was never a satisfactory arrangement, but one which Newham had inherited from the old approved school regime and, in 1974, accepted as adequate. The new development plans, with a vastly increased residential child care staff, at last means that the house units can now be open for twenty-four hours of every day.

It was decided to add two extra staff to Shackleton, by taking the relief housemaster and basing him permanently in the house and moving one of the housemothers to Shackleton. Later, Shackleton's housemother was redesignated assistant matron but still kept very much concerned with the work of the house. A careful perusal was also made of the teachers who carried out approximately fifteen hours per week extraneous duty. Two were voluntarily transferred to the house due for the influx of difficult boys.

The housewarden and I planned carefully the numerical rundown of boys in the house. We went through the records of every boy and had a clear picture of the boys likely to be left behind when we started to admit the 'hard-core' group. Some boys left naturally, and one or two moved to other houses. The remaining boys were encouraged to assist not only in decorating the house, but in choosing wallpaper and furniture. When the first of the new group moved into the house, there were five 'old-stagers' left and, as mentioned

31

previously, they were of considerable advantage to the implementation of the new scheme.

Shackleton House consisted of: *Downstairs*—one common room, one large dining room cum games room, a central office, various storecupboards, sewing room, and toilet; *upstairs*—five single bedrooms and five bedrooms for four boys each, staff sleeping-in room, toilets, bathroom and showers. The general state of decoration was poor and the furniture dilapidated.

By various means we obtained odd items of furniture and carpets. The boys and staff decorated and converted one of the bedrooms into an extra common room. The storecupboards were cleaned out and two of them taken over as a dartsroom and a disco room. I obtained four new half-size snooker tables and gave one to each house. One boy who was skilful with a paintbrush and also studying for 'A' level Art, painted a few murals on various internal walls which brightened the place up considerably. By the time the first boy was admitted, there was a distinct improvement in the material layout of Shackleton. The boys and staff had worked very hard and their efforts were more than justified.

Planning the programme

It was thought advisable to break down the future planning procedures into distinct, but overlapping, patterns, viz:

1   Senior level consultation with Shackleton staff.
2   Regular meetings with the boys alone and with staff and with boys together from Shackleton House.
3   Discussions with the heads of the Regional Assessment Centres about what Ardale hoped to do.
4   Planned and programmed discussions with individual staff from Shackleton about their particular roles.
5   A planned programme of research and testing by myself and my social caseworker.
6   Planned discussions with certain teachers regarding individual educational programmes for the boys.
7   To run small seminars for those staff concerned on the basic skills of counselling, group work, and behaviour modification.
8   To formulate individual treatment programmes for each boy and to discuss these with the staff concerned before the boy was actually admitted.
9   To personally adminster some tests but to monitor all of them and keep comprehensive records.
10   To stress flexibility to the staff and to assure them that

making mistakes initially is not necessarily anything to worry about.

11 To personally make sure that the social worker of every boy admitted into the experimental group is aware of what we are trying to do.

12 To begin admitting boys into the experimental group and to try to form a comparison group in the other three houses by admitting other boys at roughly the same period.

4   Preparing the staff for the experiment

Discussing staff roles in the new set-up

In the Curtis Report residential workers were described thus: 'The qualifications to be aimed at are personal suitability and a deep interest in children'. This is rather a dismissive approach and was not one to be exclusively fostered in the late 1970s—there should be much more emphasis on skills and attitudes. In late 1974, one of the primary functions of staff who would be dealing with the difficult boys shortly to be admitted to Ardale was an ability and aptitude to attempt to develop within the boys the strengths needed to eventually take responsibility for their own lives. They would need to help the boys to control their own emotions, evaluate any situation they may find themselves in, and act in a manner that brought positive reward to themselves and yet was not detrimental to people about them.

With this in mind, I began to hold various meetings with the staff from Shackleton to discuss such topics as key workers, group work, positive reward systems, and report writing. It was decided that each boy should have one particular member of staff to whom he could relate and would find the time to act in a personal counselling capacity. This would be his key worker.

Although this was nothing new and had been used for many years, it was necessary to look carefully at the whole system of who would counsel who. There were three distinct variables:

1 Should a key worker be chosen for a boy before he arrives so that this person plays a major role in the process of admission?
2 Should a boy be allowed to choose or gravitate towards one particular member of staff when he feels the need?
3 Should a boy be told on admission that he must choose a member of staff to be his key worker or, if not on admission, within a few weeks of his arrival?

All alternatives had advantages and disadvantages. In the end, it was decided to initially work on 1 but so closely monitor the system that it would soon be obvious if a boy particularly related to any other member of the staff. If this was the case, that person would take over the counselling role. We decided not to specifically tell the boys that one particular member of staff was acting in this capacity so that we could observe the interaction of relationships.

The position of the teachers in the house as key workers was discussed and I decided to include them in the scheme, well knowing that it was very likely that the boys would, in the first instance, relate better to those staff with whom they spent most time in a non-working situation. Both teachers agreed that they were willing to act in this capacity, but felt that they should be used only when necessary or when a particular boy formed a close relationship.

Training staff as key workers

After two general meetings with the staff concerned and numerous talks with my social caseworker, we decided to go through numerous books and draw up a list of 'dos' and 'don'ts' which, although not in any way a set of rules, would be a guideline to staff until they had developed their individual techniques. Each member of staff concerned, then, was given a copy of the following:

Aids to counselling*

1   Never adopt an authorative role; be an interested person who wants to listen to what is said.

2   Communicate by transmitting ideas and feelings; do this by being yourself and not putting on an act.

3   Try and arrange the physical setting to suit the particular boy and only use a formal setting when absolutely necessary.

4   Let the boy do most of the talking; this will show that you are interested in what he has to say.

5   Ask questions which cannot be answered by 'yes' or 'no'. (Not 'Do you like your mother'; rather 'Tell me about your mother'.)

6   Do not sound like an interrogator.

7   Do not interrupt the boy when he is talking. If he digresses focus him back on the subject.

8   Give him silence in which to think.

9   Move the focus from intellectual thought to emotional feelings when feelings are being discussed. Ask such questions as: 'How did you feel about that?'

10   Observe and try to interpret non-verbal communication.

11   Be alert to change in speech, rate, pitch, volume. Such changes may indicate that there are emotional feelings connected with the subject being discussed which may need further

*These aids were gleaned from practical experience of ourselves and other practitioners.

exploration at a later date.

12 Help the boy to be aware of what is currently happening.

13 Use brief, simple sentences.

14 Allow time for the boy to interject.

15 Allow the boy self determination. Do not give lectures on how to behave.

16 Focus on the boy's experience—not your own.

17 Clarify and interpret what he is saying, or make a summarising remark after he has finished.

18 Do not be alarmed at remarks made; instead look at the reasons behind them.

19 Never give superficial reassurance nor make promises which cannot definitely be kept.

20 Never moralise. Should the boy's conversation be full of profanities and swear words, remember that this is how most of them speak to each other. If you keep reminding him of his bad language you may as well give up for all the good you will do the boy.

21 Communicate feelings but do not get emotionally involved nor attempt to assume the boy's problem.

22 Avoid undue flattery and praise. Ask instead what the boy thinks about a certain action he may have mentioned.

23 Do not reject the boy through remarks or non-verbal clues. Do not threaten or belittle him.

24 Understand that his values may be those of his family; if you make disparaging remarks about them, you also appear to be attacking those he is closest to.

25 Refer more serious cases and discuss them with other staff in the house. Remember that occasionally confidentiality can be carried too far and may, in certain cases, be actually detrimental to a boy.

Discussing group counselling with staff

Bearing in mind the old axiom that 'a little learning is a dangerous thing', we were aware of the problems to the boys of badly organised and conducted groups, and the traumatic experience it could be to some of the staff. In the end, I decided to initially run a psychotherapeutic group myself, but to include other staff as observers. This did not, however, mean that the house group was to be the only one in operation in Shackleton House. There was considerable ignorance of group work, even amongst trained and qualified residential workers. After numerous meetings and discussions, it was decided that, initially at least, we would concentrate on four types of groupings: house task groups; psychotherapeutic groups; behaviour modification groups; educational modification groups. We ruled out suggestions of encounter and touch therapy groups and resisted the suggestion of one of the staff to institute a regression group. We did not feel competent to handle the very considerable problems of re-building a boy after total regression had been reached.

House task groups

This rather ambiguous phrase was chosen to cover a multiplicity of ideas. We had already started a group by our frequent meetings and discussions with the remaining boys in the house. Not only had they had their say about such matters as redecorating, choosing furniture, etc., but they had been listened to and some of their ideas used. In the end, the definition of task groups was put into three specific areas.

House staff groups. The staff in the 'hard-core' house would need much greater support than the staff in the other houses and would need to meet fairly frequently to formally discuss their work, problems and findings with each other. Naturally, there would be informal meetings but it was felt necessary to timetable in a definite period when all the staff could meet with my deputy and/or I present or not as the staff desired. We ruled out the idea of a weekly meeting between myself and the housewarden as it was felt that this should be seen to be a total staff team meeting.

A defined task group meeting. These were to be group meetings of boys and staff—not necessarily total boys or total staff—to discuss on-going house needs. The aim was to get the group thinking and working collectively to produce, purchase, or obtain something for the benefit of all members of the group. Within a very short time of the first meeting, there were regular delegations of boys and staff to persuade me replace the black and white television set with a colour version. When I explained that it was not (at that time) Newham's policy to provide colour sets, they set about working out all alternatives to provide their own. In the end, the housewarden transferred his own colour set to the house when there was anything special they all wanted to watch.

Policy meetings. A polite way of saying that most of these meetings began by one of the staff saying something to the effect of: 'Who stole a packet of cigarettes from the office desk?' or: 'Who put chewing-gum up the bathroom taps?' etc.

The initial aim was to give the boys the opportunity to discuss any house matter they did not like or felt was unfair, such as why they went home less frequently than many boys from the other houses. However, this never really worked out for two main reasons: firstly, the fact that the boys soon realised that these groups were only called regarding some form of misbehaviour on their part, and secondly, the success of the psychotherapeutic groups which offered a much better floor for matters of this nature.

Psychotherapeutic groups

Bion originated this type of group situation in which the group, guided by a person with some knowledge of psycho-analysis, sets the task, not of discussing a particular topic, or accomplishing an overt task, but of studying its own process of member interaction. The theory being that the group gradually learns to recognise and to deal with the latent bonds of hostility and affection which exist within it.

Having been involved before as a group member and a group conductor, I was aware that a CH(E) is not the ideal setting to hold such groups as the tide of feelings in such a group could rise to unmanageable proportions. It was mainly for this reason I decided to conduct these groups myself so that, if absolutely necessary, I could switch off and become the typical headmaster again.

Obviously, many staff were sceptical of the value of this type of group and some were aware that there would be many occasions when the boys would be discussing with the principal and amongst themselves particular weaknesses of individual members of staff. To avert this fear to some extent, group psychotherapy was defined as a form of treatment based on the consequences which follow when the same group (boys and staff) meet together regularly over a fairly long period of time, with the goal of obtaining possible attitude and personality awareness and even change. Details of these findings are described in more detail in following chapters.

Behaviour modification groups

Delinquency, being one form of deviant behaviour, should be capable of being modified. This was the hypothesis used when it was decided to incorporate some definite form of behaviour modification techniques into the treatment of the 'hard-core' group. Considerable reading and background research was carried out, culminating in a paper produced by the principal and issued to all the staff concerned.

The next few pages consist of this paper in its entirety, which is culled from experience and the relevant literature.

A paper presented to the Ardale staff in September, 1974.

An outline of behaviour modification

If we are to try and help the boys being admitted to Ardale we should try and be aware of some of the causes for the behaviour that sent them here in the first place. We must also look at the various methods of behaviour modification and try to form some method or methods to help the boys to alter their criminal life style when they leave us. I know that it is easy to say but very difficult indeed to do. Even if we gain some measure of success, it could be many years before we know and, with the present system of follow-up when a boy leaves, we may never know at all.

I must stress that although behaviour modification theories are not new they have not, to the best of my knowledge, been carried out in any depth in a CH(E). This means that we could be working in the dark to some extent. My personal views, which I hope most of you will share, are that if we cannot attempt something to lower the rate of further criminality and reconviction after a boy leaves Ardale we are failing in our job. Out present methods, which are not basically very different from when I first entered the approved school service, have a modicum of success with many boys but I feel that we could help many more if we could only, somehow, modify behaviour.

Most of us are controlled by the thought of getting caught. It is my theory that the same applies to most of our boys, but perhaps not all. There are a small number who could be classed as psychotic or moral imbeciles, but these rarely come through our hands. Most of the boys we work and live with have the same active conscience as we have but, in some cases, have come to accept getting caught as an almost occupational hazard. Most of the time they live for today and don't care about tomorrow. If we can break into this pattern I feel we can do something valuable.

Let us, for a moment, consider some of the methods of behaviour modification we will not be using. Just over a hundred years ago the hangman's rope certainly modified behaviour for theft. Similarly, long periods of incarceration modify behaviour but only by circumstances and not desire. Imprisonment does not prevent internal brutality. I must make it clear that I regard imprisonment essential in some cases for the protection of society but it does not really modify behaviour. Do not forget that there are many people who regard a CH(E) as being little different from a prison. The use of certain drugs such as chlorpromazine which can calm schizophrenics, or phenobarbitone which will reduce anxiety can help to give a definite improvement in social and other behaviour. The only problem, here, however is that they seem to be short lasting and do not make a long term or permanent alteration in behaviour.

Some theories of behaviour modification

Obviously if we intend to formulate some working theory of our own at Ardale we must look at the ideas of previous researchers. There has been quite a lot written, but mainly in a clinical sense. Here are four definitions:

> Behaviour modification is the application of knowledge from experimental psychology with animals applied to humans and mixed with a lot of scientifically stated common sense. (Poteet, 1970)

> The use of learning theory principles to alter maladaptive behaviour. (Whitman, 1971)

> The management of behaviour through the manipulation of the environment. (Chaffin and Kroth, 1971)

> Treatment techniques derived from the theories of learning and aimed at the direct modification of one or more problem behaviours rather than effecting more general and less observable personality or adjustment changes. (Gelfand and Hartmann, 1968)

The above definitions are mainly based on the medical model and the behaviour learning model of reinforcement used in the study of behaviour modifications. There are two broad classifications of behaviour which evolved from the work of Pavlov, Watson, Skinner, Thorndike and Hull—namely respondent and operant behaviour.

Respondent behaviours (also called reflex behaviour) is that behaviour in which responses are strengthened or weakened primarily by stimuli that precede the response. A typical example is the reduction in the size of the pupil of the eye when a bright light is presented. The bright light (stimulus) preceded the reduction of the size of the pupil (response).

Operant behaviour is the other broad classification. The individual operates upon his environment to produce a certain event. A boy in class raises his hand (operates upon his environment) and the teacher asks him what he wants (produces an event). Taken to extremes, the practice of operant conditioning becomes brainwashing.

Positive reinforcement is merely a complex way of saying that operant conditioning can be best achieved with some form of reward.

A boy keeps his room tidy and is rewarded with a 'well done'. Negative reinforcement, on the other hand, is the issuing of some form of physical or verbal punishment. The use of positive and negative reinforcements can be the basis of a token reward system, but my personal view is that the type of boy we are likely to be admitting into Ardale is likely to be too sophisticated, old and worldly wise to operate an effective token reward system. However, it may be worth discussing at some future meeting.

In a few short paragraphs I have tried to show you that there appears to be many methods of behaviour modification. Let us now concentrate on what we can do at Ardale with the 'hard-core' delinquent, who expresses aggression, tension, lack of emotional concern, and seems determined not to be helped or changed by anybody.

What can we do at Ardale to modify behaviour?

1 Learn observation evaluation techniques. In other words, listen, look and note. Too often we look at a broad spectrum of events without seeing the wood for the trees. Go into the dining room and watch the different methods of eating. Note the responses to situations. It can be quite rewarding to overhear a boy say: 'He doesn't miss much, does he?'

2 Regard any boy you will be acting as key worker to as the one you hope to help by various means, including the modification of his behaviour. Study his file and case notes. Make your own dossier on him if you wish but do not let the lad be aware of this. Talk to him about his behaviour and discuss with him why he acts like he does. Once you have gained his confidence— and he will definitely test you by telling deliberate lies to see if they get passed to other staff—you will begin to learn aspects of his character you may be able to use to his benefit at a later date. Do not rely on your memory. Write down the information you have discovered as soon as you are on your own.

3 Study the interaction of the peer group and use it to your advantage. A natural pecking order is bound to be created. Make sure that you know who is top dog and let him know that you will only accept this situation so long as the position is not misused.

4 Use positive reinforcement. For example: 'You can stay up and watch Match of the Day, but not until the dining room has been swept out'. In his book *Parents are Teachers*, W. C. Becker refers to this form of reinforcement as 'Grandma's rule'. Be careful that positive reinforcements do not become bribes, e.g.: 'If you don't

cause me any bother tonight, I'll let you stop up and watch Match of the Day'. A reward and a bribe are two completely different things.

5   Do not be frightened to use negative reinforcement. When a positive reinforcement is taken away or when a negative reinforcer is used, we have what is known as punishment. We all know what an emotive word this is and immediately conjure up pictures of cringing kids and brutal staff waving canes. We must learn to say 'No'. Many of our lads have always got their own way with parents, teachers and social workers by expressing such violent or anti-social behaviour when their personal desires have not been gratified that they need to learn—and learn quickly—that there are certain rules and regulations, the breaking of which will bring a negative reinforcer. Some of you may find this a difficult field of operations as it can alter relationships and trust.

6   Be aware that what works with one boy may not work with another. For example, sending a boy for a shower may be a reward for one and a punishment for another.

7   Be aware of and willing to use modelling. Some boys will model themselves on their peers, footballers, pop stars, famous villains, even you. Apart from the latter, in which a tricky path must be trod, pick out the better aspects of the model and use these to impress upon the boy the need to alter his behaviour to live up to his hero. You may have to listen to music not always to your personal taste if a pop singer is the model, but it always pays to carry out some basic research into the subject of the model. The mere fact that you are showing interest may help to improve behaviour. Some of it is hard going but remember you can find something positive in whoever the model is.

8   If you can create a genuine relationship, you will be able to talk to a boy on a relaxed one to one basis. I frequently do this by appearing to be controversial. For example, if I know a boy supports a particular football team, I will set up a situation to discuss with another boy, but in the hearing of the boy I want to get through to, the merits of a different football team, running down the team I know the boy supports. It is not very often that he will be able to resist joining in the conversation. It is then up to you to steer it away from football and to the subject you want, e.g. football to football hooliganism to hooliganism in general to violence to an act of violence committed by the boy.

9   At all times—even when you have to count to ten—set an example. You may have to raise your voice at times and you may have to break up an act of violence between two boys by grabbing

both of them and pulling them apart. You may have to physically defend yourself from attack and even use justifiable physical restraint. But do not get yourself a reputation of always shouting, nagging, or being the hard man that other staff have to call out. If you do, you are in danger of losing any form of relationship and, although you may be feared, you will not be respected. If we are going to modify boys' behaviour, we must make sure that our own does not need modifying too often.

10 Behaviour can be modified by the use of the right stimulus. How often have we heard a boy say: 'I did it because I was bored'? I know that a few boys would be bored after a time if I provided a bar and a brothel in the school, but this is no reason why we should not seek an individual stimulus for each boy. Try to locate and develop any latent skills a boy may have. If it is possible to share a skill with a boy so much the better. We will never completely remove all the boredom of a residential school, especially at the weekends. Let us, however, try to reduce it as much as possible.

Evaluating what we do

Much of the formal evaluation will be carried out by myself, but your help is very much needed. There are a number of ways we can carry out evaluation. One will be to compare baseline data with data obtained after the project has begun. This can only be done if a continuous recording of behaviour takes place. The graphing of recording makes the comparison a simple task. This type of evaluation is generally called the ABAB design, or the reversal design. The baseline data is termed A, and during the programme data is termed B. A is compared to B to note any change. Then the reinforcement programme is terminated to revert to the baseline conditions of A. The programme is begun again and data for B is obtained. I know that this may sound rather complicated but when you see the behaviour graphed, you will become aware of the influence you personally may be having on a particular boy's behaviour. Another system I may be using is called the multiple baseline design, but it is a little more complicated and not really necessary to describe here.

In all research programmes of this nature, there are a number of pitfalls such as maturation, instrumentation, regression effects and selection. It is for this reason that I will personally carry out a number of programmes and cross refer the findings. It will be of considerable benefit if we are able to modify the behaviour of some of the boys at Ardale. It will be of even more benefit if we can statistically show that we are able to do this.

The above paper was presented by myself to a select group of staff concerned with my 'hard-core' experiment at Ardale.

Educational modification groups

Although modifying educational progress and/or behaviour was only another branch of behaviour modification, we decided to treat it, as far as the teachers were concerned, as a separate field. The two teachers used with the 'hard-core' group both felt that they had developed their own skills of class control. Like all teachers, they had been basically trained to help the normal child. There are very few teacher training courses which give practical and useful advice in dealing with the classroom thug. Many of the boys in our experiment had been excluded from a number of previous schools, including schools for maladjusted boys. Having taught in what is loosely referred to as a normal school, as well as special and approved schools, I was aware of the set up whereby head teachers make much less of a fuss when their disruptive pupils regularly truant than they do with the more placid child. Some of the boys we had to try and help had missed as much as two full years schooling by the time they were fifteen. Many of them had obtained unofficial jobs and were earning money. This, of course, does not only apply to the 10 per cent 'hard-core' child, but to the majority of boys admitted to CH(E)s. Those critics of CH(E)s should realise that the basic material we have does not, in the main, have any desire to continue formal education and many are openly opposed to the idea.

For the reasons stated above, it was decided to concentrate on more vocational training, using the academic side as a rough basis for every boy and a concentrated programme for those boys with the ability and inclination to take formal academic examinations. The basic argument has always been that a CH(E) is more likely to produce more carpenters than nuclear physicists; therefore it should concentrate its resources on the woodwork department rather than the science laboratory. Some will argue that this is wrong, but practical experience has taught otherwise. Vocational training became a dirty phrase when approved schools became CH(E)s. This vogue has now reversed and many social workers are seeking places in CH(E)s which give basic trade training.

There were one or two of Ardale's teachers who felt that a relatively unstructured programme of work was what was needed with the boys. With a few, this may have been so, but for the majority an unstructured educational programme only increased insecurity and placed responsibilities on shoulders that were not equipped to carry them. To allow pressures and anxieties to build up by using various avoidance techniques usually produced no work of any kind. Permissiveness was certainly not the answer for the 'hard-core' group.

Ideally, it was desirable to have small teaching groups outside the classroom area, probably in the boys' house units, but staffing problems made this very difficult. The first deputy did take a small group of boys away from the schoolroom area for what he called 'having fun with maths', but he was a very special and experienced kind of teacher.

It was felt that if we were going to evaluate educational progress with the 'hard-core' group, we must also run a comparison group. Accordingly, the same two teachers, with a certain amount of assistance, ran a similar group (size, age, IQ, etc.) for the same number of periods per week with the boys admitted normally.

Experience has led me to believe that, when given the opportunity to choose any type of behaviour to modify, most teachers choose to work first on behaviour that disrupts the class. With small groups this was less of a concern, although aggressive behaviour was a problem. It was necessary to persuade the teachers that classroom behaviour modification was a philosophy or technique with a positive orientation and that it could be used to increase as well as decrease behaviour. It is rather unfortunate that most teachers think of decreasing behaviour rather than increasing it, viz:

Decreasing behaviour	Increasing behaviour
stop fighting	get along with peers
stop running round class	stay in seat more often
stop swearing	use more acceptable words
stop interrupting	raise hand more often.

Diagnostic or prescriptive teaching

All good teachers ask themselves why a particular child is not learning. Typical answers given to them might say because he is emotionally disturbed, is mentally retarded, has a learning difficulty, or some such response. Such labelling does not give the teacher any direction for instruction. Perhaps the question should not be why isn't a boy learning but how does he learn? Only after this question is answered can an appropriate instruction take place. Diagnostic/prescriptive (D/P) teaching provides a framework within which a teacher can determine how a boy learns and subsequently choose appropriate instructional strategies to use with him. D/P teaching is an ongoing process wherein instructional strategies are matched to the boy's unique learning mode. A learning mode is that pattern of relationships among input, process, and output which serves to effect desired behavioural change.

The D/P teacher must integrate information received from many different sources with the information he receives from his own informal diagnostic activities to answer the questions of *how* a boy learns. It was found necessary to devise certain diagnostic tests for the teachers to administer in the first instance, although they managed to elaborate and improve these as their experience increased.

Teaching by objectives

Most teachers, particularly those tied down to any form of examination schedule, state that (a) they have not got enough time to cover the whole syllabus, and (b) the lads do not seem to assimilate what is taught them. It was decided that 'hard-core' and comparison groups should work along these lines and the teachers concerned should think about the following sequence:

1 State your objectives in as specific terms as possible, e.g.:
'Today we are going to learn the metric system'. Explain why.
2 Note any special problems that you will have to overcome,
e.g. one boy cannot measure in feet and inches so that will
have to be revised first.
3 Assess what resources you will require, e.g. have you got
sufficient metric rulers. Can you obtain job descriptions for
builders, etc. which state the need to know the metric system.
Have you any plans to show the use of the metric system in
industry?
4 State the programme of work that seems most likely to
surmount or evade the problems and achieve the objectives with
the available resources, e.g. plan to measure part of the school
grounds in metres and resist the temptation to go wandering off
all over London with rulers handy but boys probably missing.
5 Evaluate the success of the programme, with a view to revising
it or the objectives if necessary. Boys may be far more interested
in relating the metric system to possible future employment than
walking around the school measuring corridors. In simple terms,
keep records, be flexible, and learn from any initial mistakes you
will probably make.

The need to have a flexible approach

The sterile formal teaching which many of us over the age of forty experienced as children would not, I know, be the right approach with the experimental group. Most of them had been through, and rejected, this system at least once in their lives prior to being admitted to Ardale.

Obviously 'play' is relative: conkers for one boy of fifteen, chess for another. One of the most successful maths groups we had run at Ardale was when we entered the Daily Mail Bridge Competition. Admittedly we never got past the second round, but this, I regarded, as better maths teaching than all the formal book work. The boys did not even regard it as school work, but many of them worked harder than they had ever done sitting behind a desk doing sums.

Interest plays a major part in the learning process. Thus, it is logical that teachers should be aware of the interests of boys in order that the learning and performance of desired practices might be enhanced. As far back as 1937, C. C. Cowell wrote: 'Knowledge of those activities in which children tend to participate joyously and spontaneously of their own volition seems indispensable to sound educational philosophy and method. (Cowell, 1937)

One of the main points it was necessary to get over to the teachers was the need to know what each boy was interested in and base some lessons around these subjects. From a simple interest in a specific football team, can evolve, English, maths, history, geography, etc., all without the boy knowing he is really going through a fairly normal learning process.

Planning the special education group

The first task was to try to break down the boys' view of the classroom as a foreign and hostile environment. The obvious answer was to attempt to discover in each individual case what was causing anxiety and trauma and try to eliminate it. At Ardale we have certain advantages over larger school establishments. The smaller building is not so intimidating or overwhelming as many of the huge comprehensive schools with which we burden our children. There are fewer teachers with whom the boys have to make relationships, and these teachers have access to papers giving a detailed history of every boy. The two specific teachers chosen had time to attend to each boy individually and the knowledge to treat each boy with sympathy and understanding. The smallness of the group was an invaluable asset as the teacher could afford to be relaxed and friendly and still

47

maintain discipline. He could encourage questions and requests for help. He had time for the individual; consequently each boy worked separately in his own time and there was little competition between him and others in the class.

The more experienced teachers were aware that, probably above all, boys fear being shown up, given work which is beyond their capabilities and feeling foolish and inferior. It makes no difference that they are relatively intelligent individuals and 'hard-core' juvenile delinquents. There is a marked discrepancy between a boy's impression of himself and his actual achievements. To avoid creating feelings of inferiority in the boy he was initially given work which was well within his capabilities. As far as possible, a situation was created in which failure was well nigh impossible. A boy would be given very simple routine tasks, so easy that he could not fail. He was allowed to continue with this type of work for as long as he wished. It was known that he would indicate soon enough when he was ready to move on. This was one of the most difficult things to get over to some of the teachers who felt that the art of teaching was to cram in as much as possible as quickly as possible. In the end, however, they saw that the new methods were working.

During the settling in period, new boys from the 'hard-core' group observed the teacher very closely and the weighing up process began. At this point the behaviour of the teacher was a paramount importance. Long discussions were held with the teachers to make them aware that the boys were looking to see that each of them could be trusted to do the following:

1 To behave consistently.
2 To maintain control and discipline. Teachers have to set definite limits over which a boy cannot step without just retribution. An over lenient teacher who does not give clear guidelines produces insecurity. He must be able to control the worst bully in the class so that in the teacher's company even the puniest weakling feels safe. For this reason, unsupervised interludes were cut down to a bare minimum.
3 He must be fair and behave equally to every boy.
4 He must not embarrass, but provide situations in which a boy can feel like others and not different from them.
5 He must aim at establishing a good working relationship with the boys.
6 He must give clear directions and make known exactly what is required of every boy.
7 He must be adept at avoiding power struggles. He must be able to recognise danger signals very early and by tact, humour and common sense to refuse to allow a situation to develop.

8 He must be completely unflappable and unshockable. He needs to be sufficiently accepting to be able to take abnormal behaviour in his stride.

9 He must be able to recognise the boy's need for approval and to give it on every occasion available. Showing too much disappointment in work produced is often seen as failure by the boys.

When a good teacher-pupil relationship is established and the boy gains enough confidence to be ready to progress academically, he can then embark on a very carefully planned programme of work. He can progress slowly and be edged forward very gently.

Consultation with individual social workers

Although this is not strictly relevant to training and helping staff to accept the 'hard-core' experiment, it was thought advisable to give some help to social workers of the boys admitted to the experiment. Obviously it was not possible to inform every social worker and no specific information was given to the social workers of boys admitted normally. It was thought, however, that the word would quickly get around from the Regional Assessment Centres that Ardale was willing to try and help some boys other establishments had refused.

The normal procedure when agreeing to accept a boy was, after very carefully going through the assessment reports, to write to the social worker stating that Ardale was prepared to admit the boy and if he or she phoned we could either arrange an admittance date or a time when he or she could visit. A copy of this letter was sent to the Regional Assessment Centre for their information.

It was felt, however, that we must give social workers more general information about Ardale and what we had to offer. Unfortunately it was not until mid 1975 that we actually got around to producing our two brochures—one for social workers and one for parents. In retrospect, it is quite clear that we should have involved the social workers of the 'hard-core' group much more right from the beginning. We should have insisted that they visit Ardale in advance and discuss the mutual problems we all had to face up to. We should have also tried to have much more initial contact with the parents. Probably in this area, more than anything else the planning was weak.

With the boys accepted into my 'hard-core' group, the same letter was sent to every social worker as follows:

> I have recently received the assessment papers on the above-named boy from the Regional Assessment Centre at ... In

most cases I accept a boy unconditionally, but in the case of ..... I can only initially offer a place on a two-month trial period, and I could not accept him until I have this confirmed by you in writing.

If during or at the end of the two-month trial period it is thought that Ardale is the wrong placement for the boy or the boy is unable to fit into the normal routine, I would wish to hold a Case Conference here with you and your Senior present to discuss alternative placement. If the boy settles here and takes advantage of what we have to offer, I still wish to hold a Case Review at Ardale and make the placement here permanent until it is thought by all concerned that he is ready to leave.

The reason(s) for accepting him only initially for a trial period of two months is (are) as follows:

If you agree to this arrangement, as soon as I receive a letter of confirmation from you I will telephone you and arrange a date for you to visit, if you desire, or a speedy date of entry for the boy.

We can all look back at our mistakes and it can be stated quite categorically that now we insist on seeing not only the social worker but the senior and maybe the area officer as well before we admit a boy. We also insist that the boy visits in advance—not to decide whether or not he wants to come, but to have a look around and meet the staff.

Statistics speak for themselves. Of the fifty boys accepted into the 'hard-core' experiment, only 4 (8 per cent) of the social workers visited prior to the boy being admitted, although 7 (14 per cent) knew Ardale by having another boy on their case load here at some time or another.

5 Pre-admission facts and details

What is assessment?

The purpose of assessment is to provide a sound and diagnostic basis on which to provide effective treatment and to attempt to place a child appropriately so that, as far as possible, his first placing will be his last. Clause 34 (4b) of the 1969 Children and Young Persons Act states: 'Regional Plans should contain proposals for facilities for observation of children in the care of relevant authorities and for the assessment of the most suitable accommodation and treatment for these children'. Whatever the nomenclature adopted, 'assessment' or 'classifying' or 'observation and assessment', the function that is carried out under this heading has many elements. It includes the collection and collation from all sources of a complete dossier of historical and developmental information about the individual, his family, his education, his environment and the assumptions on which earlier treatment intervention have been based. To this is added a thorough going up to date evaluation of needs which result in a complete diagnostic recommendation for treatment. In an article published in *Child in Care,* the principal of Aycliffe CH(E), Dr M. Hoghugi, states: 'The evaluation of other people's characteristics and behaviour patterns is an essential pre-requisite to social living'.

In agreement with a decision made by the London Boroughs Childrens Regional Planning Committee (LBCRPC), the heads of CH(E)s and Directors of Social Service for the London boroughs agreed in early 1975 that no child would be admitted to a CH(E) without a full or paper assessment at one of the Regional Assessment Centres. The need for this arose in the early 1970s when, following clause 34 of the 1969 Act, there was a sudden upsurge of small, and often inefficient observation and assessment centres. Many small community homes and their controlling authorities decided that part of the function of any and almost every community home was to assess the children in their establishments.

From this free for all system arose a variety of reports and techniques. Some reports were excellent and compared very favourably with the old classifying school reports, but many were, to say the least, inadequate.

51

There was almost unanimous support of the LBCRPC suggestion that most forms of assessment for CH(E)s be standardised in some respect, certainly in the provision of basic information and history. It was also totally agreed that CH(E) heads would no longer accept boys based on reports from non-regional assessment centres. The Regional Planning Committee agreed to inspect all the assessment centres and, for those that came up to a high enough standard, grant them Regional Assessment Centre titles. From that date on, any report from other than a RAC was referred back to the sender.

It is not the aim of this work to go into great details about assessment and the preparation of assessment reports. Although one or two boys from the 'hard-core' and comparison groups were assessed, in the early days at a non-Regional Assessment Centre, the vast majority were assessed or paper assessed at two Regional Assessment Centres only—Stamford House (Shepherd's Bush) and The Royal Philanthropic (Redhill, Surrey). Towards the end of the experiment, an occasional boy was also admitted from Little Heath Lodge (Newham).

Twice the phrase 'paper assessment' has been quoted. It is perhaps necessary to clarify this and distinguish it from a full 'residential assessment'. The latter means that a boy is taken into a residential RAC for a period of approximately a month and given a battery of tests and interviews before a report is drawn up and reviews are held to decide the most appropriate placement. A paper assessment, however, is when a non-Regional Assessment Centre makes its own report on a boy and sends the report—and not the boy—to one of the RACs for allocation. The boy is usually never seen by the RAC staff, although it is almost inevitable that further information is requested before a placement review can be held. At least 98 per cent of paper assessments are considerably inferior to a full regional assessment. Those non-regional centres which are capable of producing a full and detailed report are usually given RAC status anyway.

Assessment cannot be static: it must always be on going. Much of the initial treatment programme arranged for each boy is based on the assessment report, but it is continually up dated. A running log or occurrence sheet is an integral part of every boy's file and is often referred to when preparing reports for case reviews which are, after all, only on going assessment meetings.

The remainder of this small section outlines the basic information received from the Regional Assessment Centres on the 'hard-core' group and my two comparison groups B and C as described earlier. Apart from the first section, they are shown as percentages to allow a quicker comparison to be made as the numbers in the three groups were fifty, twenty and twenty-five.

Table 5.1

Assessment details of group A—the 'hard-core' group

		%
Fully assessed at Stamford House	22	44
Paper assessed at Stamford House	3	6
Fully assessed at Redhill	16	32
Paper assessed at Redhill	4	8
Assessed elsewhere	5	10

Table 5.2

Assessment details of group B—first comparison group

		%
Fully assessed at Stamford House	8	40
Paper assessed at Stamford House	3	15
Fully assessed at Redhill	6	30
Paper assessed at Redhill	1	5
Assessed elsewhere	2	10

Table 5.3

Assessment details of group C—second comparison group

		%
Fully assessed at Stamford House	11	44
Paper assessed at Stamford House	3	12
Fully assessed at Redhill	8	32
Paper assessed at Redhill	1	4
Assessed elsewhere	2	8

Table 5.4

The assessment centre's estimates of the presenting needs

	A	B	C
1 Type of regime recommended		%	
Firmly structured	60	52	54
Liberal—easy going	8	10	10
Some structure	18	32	30
Specialised (psychiatric)	14	6	6

	A	B	C
2 Special features		%	
Persistent truancy	64	48	42
Excessive drinking	18	2	0
Physical violence	54	16	14
Aggressive behaviour	82	40	38
Drugs	8	0	0
Acute sexual problems	6	2	2
Delinquency only	0	18	16

NB: Where percentages total over 100 it is indicated that certain boys have more than one special feature.

	A	B	C
3 Educational needs			
Remedial	32	30	32
Small group	26	16	10
Normal teaching	8	20	22
Exam course	4	10	10
Not known	10	0	0
Mainly vocational	20	24	26

	A	B	C
4 Psychiatric treatment			
Regular treatment	8	0	0
Regular supervision	26	4	6
Occasional supervision	20	22	22
No treatment advocated	46	74	72

	A	B	C
5 Degree of casework with boy needed			
Intensive	50	24	28
Some	48	32	30
Normal contact	2	40	38
Minimal	0	6	4
None	0	0	0

	A	B	C
6 Initial recommended placement		%	
Home or foster home	4	14	16
Residential maladjusted school	6	10	10
Secure accommodation	8	0	0
Adolescent psychiatric unit	4	0	0
CH(E)—not specifically named	30	54	60
CH(E)—Ardale specifically named	22	10	12
CH(E)—Other specifically named	24	0	0
*Other placements	2	2	2

*Hostel, remand centre, detention centre, Borstal.

Comments on above six tables

All six tables show the remarkable similarity between groups B and C and their conjoint discrepancy with the 'hard-core' group A. This is particularly noticeable with the special features of physical violence and aggressive behaviour. It would also appear that the average type of boy going through the RACs are not best helped in a liberal and easy going atmosphere.

There is nothing very startling about the educational requirements. The figures for all three groups show that a general remedial and vocational course is the most desired and appropriate. The gap between group A's need for regular psychiatric supervision and groups B and C's need for no particular psychiatric treatment is blatantly obvious.

As is only to be expected, group A are assessed as being in far greater need for intensive casework than the other two groups who, in the main, need fairly normal contact.

As one would assume, approximately 70 per cent of all three groups are assessed as being in need of a CH(E) placement. If not, the papers would not have been sent to CH(E)s. The most startling fact to emerge, however, and one that applies to the 'hard-core' group only, is that 24 per cent of the boys who were admitted to Ardale were initially recommended—and refused by—other CH(E)s. This was one of the reasons for starting this experiment.

Table 5.5

Facts known on admission, or shortly after arrival

Note: All figures for the three groups are shown as percentages. When the numbers total over 100, e.g. previous treatment, it indicates that some boys figure in more than one category.

	A	B	C
1 Ethnic groupings			
UK and Ireland	42	54	48
Negroid type	48	38	32
Indian type	0	4	6
Half-caste	10	4	4
2 Stated religion			
Church of England (Anglican)	20	22	26
Methodist or Baptist	12	10	12
Roman Catholic	4	8	10
Jehovah Witness	2	0	4
Christian Scientist	2	0	0
Spiritualist	2	0	0
Muslim	6	0	4
Rastifarian	10	8	10
Mormon	4	0	0
None known nor stated	38	52	34
3 Number of court appearances			
None (in care only)	0	4	8
One	0	28	20
Two	0	32	30
Three	44	30	30
Four or more but less than ten	38	6	12
Over ten	18	0	0

4 Time spent in RAC after review*

*This does *not* indicate the length of assessment, but the difficulty in placement after the placement review. In later cases (1976) some boys were sent home while a place was sought but in all cases this table shows the delay between recommendation of a placement and the actual placement being taken up.

	A	B	C
One week or less	2	4	0
Two weeks	26	42	44
Up to three weeks	20	46	44
Up to four weeks	22	8	12
Up to two months	16	0	0
Over two months	14	0	0

5 Previous treatment experienced

	A	B	C
Remand centre	26	14	12
Secure accommodation	8	0	0
Detention centre	34	18	16
Clinic or hospital	8	0	0
Community home	62	44	42
Special school (maladjusted or ESN)	44	42	38
CH(E)—other than Ardale	22	4	0
Fostered	0	0	6
Supervision order	84	62	64
At home on care order	28	84	88
None listed	0	4	0

6 Age when first taken into care

	A	B	C
Under ten	20	8	6
Ten to twelve	26	12	16
Thirteen	38	42	40
Fourteen	16	34	28
Fifteen	0	4	6
Sixteen	0	0	4

7 The offences committed*

*It is essential to show both those sets of figures together. If we merely showed the committal offences, it could be falsely deduced, for example, that the 'hard-core' group never steal cars.

	Last court Appearance			Other court Appearances		
	A	B	C	A	B	C
Abusive behaviour	0	4	8	10	14	12
Assault (common)	10	0	0	42	16	18
Actual bodily harm	10	0	0	38	8	6
Beyond control	0	18	16	32	30	38
Breach of previous order	0	10	18	56	54	48
Buggery	0	0	0	4	0	4
Burglary and attempted burglary	16	10	6	48	46	52
Breaking and entering (theft)	0	0	0	56	84	78
Causing an affray	0	0	0	4	4	0
Causing unnecessary suffering	0	0	0	6	0	0
Criminal damage	6	0	6	32	18	26
Demanding with menaces	0	0	0	16	0	0
Destroy by fire (arson)	4	0	0	12	0	4
Discharge of firearm	0	0	0	10	0	0
Drink offences	0	8	0	46	38	28
Forgery	0	0	0	0	4	0
Fraud	0	0	6	0	8	12
Grievous bodily harm	12	0	0	28	0	0
Gross indecency	0	0	0	4	4	0
Handling stolen goods	2	10	0	30	40	38
Indecent assault	0	0	0	10	0	0
Incest	0	0	0	2	0	0
Larceny (petty)—shoplifting	6	10	4	82	64	66
Menacing telephone calls	0	0	4	2	0	0
Possession of drugs	4	4	0	18	10	10
Possession of firearms	4	0	0	22	0	0
Rape and attempted rape	2	0	0	12	0	4
Receiving stolen goods	0	10	12	28	34	38
Road traffic act offences	8	10	4	64	60	72
Robbery and armed robbery	4	0	0	12	4	0
Taking and driving away	0	6	8	64	64	68
Trespass with intent to steal	8	0	0	16	18	20
Other offences	4	0	8	16	18	20

8 Basic IQ as shown by previous testing

These figures merely show the IQ, for what it is worth, as recorded for the three groups at Ardale who took part in the 'hard-core' experiment. Most of the results are obtained by the use of the Wechsler Intelligence Scale for Children (WISC). The rating of the British Psychological Society (BPS) is given as well as the Intelligence Quotient (IQ). It must be remembered that throughout the whole duration of the experiment, Ardale had a criterion for admission based on boys of at least average intelligence.

Intelligence Quotient	BPS rating	A	B	C
131- 45	Superior	10	8	8
116- 30	Above average	24	20	22
106- 15	High average	36	40	42
95-105	Average	24	24	24
85- 94	Low average	6	8	4
70- 84	Below average	0	0	0
55- 69	Educationally sub-normal	0	0	0
Below 55	Severely sub-normal	0	0	0

9 Educational testing prior to admission

	A	B	C
Reading age above chronological age	32	28	26
Reading age commensurate to chronological age	28	34	36
Reading age below chronological age	18	26	24
Reading age not known	22	12	16
Arithmetic age above chronological age	4	6	6
Arithmetic age commensurate to chronological age	18	24	20
Arithmetic age below chronological age	52	62	64
Arithmetic age not known	26	8	10

The better regional assessment reports also provide details of psychiatric and psychological testing and interview notes. Occasionally we also receive details of personality ratings.

Numerous details—usually in the form of a pen picture—are given in connection with family and criminal involvement. As these are dealt with in some greater detail later in this work, it is sufficient to note in this section that such information is available and is usually provided.

One of the failings of assessment centre reports is the lack of information as to exactly what CH(E) they have already been touted around to before being sent to Ardale for consideration. This is, as part of the experiment, very necessary information as it gives some indication of the apparent reasons boys were being refused at other CH(E)s.

Notes from above statistics

The obvious similarity in findings between the three groups at Ardale is quite interesting. As stated earlier, we tried to use comparison groups of boys in the same age, IQ, and general range but at the time, obviously, had no access to the overall statistics we now have at the end of the experiment.

The only point of note, and it may mean nothing from the three small samples used, in relation to ethnic groupings is that there were considerably more half-caste boys in the 'hard-core' sample. Children of mixed marriages appear to have and be more problem than their peers of either white or black parents. They are often rejected by both main ethnic groups, although it is customary at Ardale for a half-caste boy not only to relate himself to the black groupings, but to be much more anti-white than his negroid peers.

Very few assessment reports even bother to state a boy's religion and most of the information in Table 5.5 (2), has been gleaned from direct questioning of a boy and/or his parents. For the sake of convenience, included in the 'none known' section are two who claim to be satanists or devil worshippers—surprisingly neither from group A!!!

The similarity between groups B and C and their dissimilarity with group A give some indication of the actual criminal difference between the 'hard-core' boy and the normal delinquent. The results, when presented boldly as in section 3 are really quite frightening. Nine boys from group A had appeared in court over ten times. Although it has not been made clear earlier, court appearances involving one or more remands have been excluded. Thus a boy may appear three or four times for the same offence, being remanded for a further period while investigations are being carried out. In all cases, this has been regarded as one court appearance.

As Ardale only admitted boys of reasonably high intelligence it was obvious that a number of boys would have educational abilities over and above their chronological age. The small samples actually show the 'hard-core' group having a higher reading ability than the other two groups. This is probably due to the small size of the samples and in no way indicates that there is a correlation between 'hard-core' and reading ability. The figures clearly outline a fact I have been preaching for years and years—the standard of arithmetic teaching in many British schools is not as high as it could be.

It is necessary to discuss the other section at this stage as the various findings are referred to in the course of the various tests and questionnaires discussed later. Perhaps the only point worthy of note at this stage relates to section 7 of table 5.5. Apart from breaches of previous orders—usually supervision orders, the main offences committed by the boys in all three samples still revolves around theft (without violence) of some kind, although the 'hard-core' group do seem to be far more involved than the others in grievous bodily harm.

The actual process of admission

Once preparation with regard to buildings, staff and procedures had been completed, on 29 August 1974, Ardale admitted its first genuine 'hard-core' boy on the two month trial experimental scheme.

This was a fifteen and a half year old half-caste boy. Extracts from his file stated:

> Constant source of disturbance and unpleasantness both in and out of the class ... Impertinent and insolent ... He has referred with pride to his exploits of paki-bashing ... We had a request from the RC Priest not to send him to Mass for a while as he was causing so much disturbance in church ... Three boys have absconded because of his bullying ... etc.

He had been excluded from two day schools and removed from two residential homes. His papers had previously been sent to two other CH(E)s who refused to admit him.

His social worker—who did not visit Ardale prior to the boy's admission—agreed by telephone that we would not indicate to the boy that he was being admitted for a trial period only. We both felt that if he was aware of this he would very likely use his past experiences to prove that he was such a disturbing factor that he would have to be removed before his two months were completed. As a matter of fact he stayed at Ardale until November 1975 (fifteen months) and then left by the normal process to take up employment.

He arrived with his social worker at 10.30 a.m. and was met by myself, my first deputy, and the senior staff of Shackleton House. I had a short chat with the boy and then took the social worker to my office to (a) find out further information and, (b) give the lad a chance to meet other boys and settle in before having to face a long talk with 'the old man'. The warden and housemother had a chat with him over a cup of coffee and showed him around the house, letting him, with some restriction, choose his own room. As arranged, one of the nucleus of boys left in the house by careful selection joined the group at 11.30 a.m. and spent the rest of the day with him. He was introduced to the teacher responsible for him in the afternoon who took him around the classrooms and workshops and discussed with him the element of the guided choice he would have in selecting what lessons he did. In the evening, the housewarden took all the boys in his house to the cinema and they sat in the school mini-bus eating fish and chips out of newspaper on the way back. In later conversation with the boy, when we got to know and trust each other, he told me that he had not expected to be received into Ardale like he was. When I asked him to be more explicit he said: 'You know, Sir, like I was kind of wanted and not just a piece of shit'. Three days later when the second boy was admitted into the experiment, virtually the same procedure was carried out, but he was given less chance of choosing his own bedroom, as it had been decided to try putting him in with the first boy admitted. It didn't work out too well and two days after his arrival, he asked to move in with one of the nucleus boys. This was readily agreed to.

In the last few pages, an attempt has been made to show the amount of care and thought that went into admitting a boy of the 'hard-core' category and how it was hoped to be able to help him. Much of the remainder of this book concerns various forms of statistical research and evaluation of the experiment which endeavour to prove—or disprove—our basic hypotheses.

6   Assessing the social climate

The initial concept of the Ardale 'hard-core' experiment was, as previously explained, practical and not basically research orientated. Although, as a matter of necessity, research was carried out and recorded, none of this was originally geared towards a detailed written account of the work and my findings. It was not until March 1975 that we felt that the scheme had been running long enough to do any in depth evaluation.

During the process of this section, I leaned very heavily on the formula, questionnaires and evaluation methods of an American researcher, Dr R. H. Moos. It must be noted that I have made considerable adaptations to his formulae so that his basic structure can be used to cope with a completely different type of study to the original.

Slightly paraphrasing Dr Moos' reasons for this type of research, (Moos, 1975 p.36), my purpose was to develop a way of assessing the social climate in Shackleton House by asking the boys and staff individually about the usual pattern of behaviour in their programme. The hope was that the information resulting from this type of assessment could be used for programming development and for on going efforts to change the living and working environment at Ardale. It was also felt that the technique might be useful in periodic assessments of the social milieu of Shackleton House, and that it might be capable of detecting or bringing to light house tensions before violent crises occurred.

To accomplish these goals it seemed important that each boy and each member of staff in Shackleton House have an opportunity to present his perceptions of the house, Ardale in general and the efforts of the experimental scheme. By using the comparison group it was possible to find out what the boys and staff in both Shackleton House and Nansen Houses thought of the experiment. I wondered if the latter were jealous. The remainder of this section deals then with the adaptation of Dr Moos Correctional Institutions Environment Scale (CIES).

The groups tested

1 March 1975	—	Ten boys from the 'hard-core' group in Shackleton House.
2 March 1975	—	Ten boys from the comparison house (Nansen).
3 March 1975	—	The five housestaff and two teachers of Shackleton House.
4 March 1975	—	The three housestaff and two teachers of Nansen House.
5 November 1975	—	As for group 1.*
6 November 1975	—	As for group 2.**
7 November 1975	—	As for group 3.
8 November 1975	—	As for group 4.

* One boy had left between March and November and was replaced in the second testing by another 'hard-core' boy.
**Similarly, one boy had left between tests and was replaced by a substitute boy for the November tests.

The questionnaire

(Administered to boys and staff in March and November 1975, and based on the CIES **short** form (form S) questionnaire by Moos)

Name   Date

Instructions

There are thirty-six statements below. You have to decide which statements are true in your house and which are not.

True   — Circle the T when you think the statement is true or mostly true of your house.

False — Circle the F when you think the statement is false or mostly false of your house.

Please make sure to answer every statement.

T	F	1 Staff have very little time to encourage boys.
T	F	2 The staff make sure that the house is always tidy.
T	F	3 Once a timetable is arranged for a boy, he must keep to it.
T	F	4 The television room is often messy.
T	F	5 Boys are expected to share their personal problems with each other.

T	F	6	The staff act on boys' suggestions and ideas;
T	F	7	Boys rarely talk about their personal problems with other boys.
T	F	8	Boys will be transferred from this house if they don't obey the rules.
T	F	9	Staff are interested in following up boys once they leave.
T	F	10	There is very little emphasis on making plans for leaving Ardale.
T	F	11	The staff help new boys get acquainted with the house.
T	F	12	The staff sometimes argue with each other.
T	F	13	If a boy's programme or timetable is changed, someone on the staff tells him why.
T	F	14	Boys are expected to take leadership in the house.
T	F	15	Boys are encouraged to show their feelings.
T	F	16	Boys are encouraged to plan for the future.
T	F	17	The boys are proud of their house.
T	F	18	All decisions about the house are made by the staff and not by the boys.
T	F	19	The more mature boys in the house help take care of the less mature ones.
T	F	20	The house usually looks a little messy.
T	F	21	Personal problems are openly discussed.
T	F	22	Boys may criticise staff members to their face.
T	F	23	Staff and boys say how they feel about each other.
T	F	24	The staff give the boys very little responsibility.
T	F	25	There is very little emphasis on what boys will be doing when they leave Ardale.
T	F	26	People say what they really think around here.
T	F	27	Boys are encouraged to learn new ways of doing things.
T	F	28	This is not a very well organised house.
T	F	29	Boys here really try to improve and get better.
T	F	30	Staff are always changing their mind here.
T	F	31	Boys tend to hide their feelings from the staff.
T	F	32	Boys in this house care about each other.
T	F	33	Discussions in the house emphasise the understanding of personal problems.
T	F	34	When boys first arrive in the house, someone shows them around and explains how the house operates.
T	F	35	There is very little group spirit in the house.
T	F	36	Boys have a say about what goes on here.

Thank you. Please make sure you have answered all the statements.

Evaluating the CIES questionnaire

With slight alterations we evaluated the findings of the above questionnaires based on nine sub-scale descriptions as outlined by R. H. Moos. (Moos, 1973) The nine sub-scales are as follows:

The CIES sub-scale descriptions

1 *Involvement* Measures how active and energetic boys are in the day to day functioning of the programme, i.e. interacting socially with other boys, doing things on their own initiative, and developing pride and group spirit in the programme.

2 *Support* Measures the extent to which boys are encouraged to be helpful and supportive towards other boys, and how supportive the staff is towards boys.

3 *Expressiveness* Measures the extent in which the programme encourages the open expression of feelings (including angry feelings) by boys and staff.

4 *Autonomy* Assesses the extent to which boys are encouraged to take initiative in planning activities and take leadership in their own house.

5 *Practical orientation* Assesses the extent to which boys' environment orients him towards preparing himself for leaving. Such things as training for new kinds of jobs, looking to the future, and working towards goals are considered.

6 *Personal problem orientation* Measures the extent to which boys are encouraged to be concerned with their personal problems and feelings, and to seek to understand them.

7 *Order and organisation* Measures how important order and organisation is in the programme, in terms of boys (how they look), staff (what they do to encourage order) and facility itself (how well it is kept).

8 *Clarity* Measures the extent to which the boy knows what to expect in the day to day programme and how explicit the programme rules and procedures are.

9 *Staff control*   Assesses the extent to which staff use measures to keep boys under necessary controls, i.e. in the formulation of rules, the scheduling of activities, and in the relationships between boys and staff.

Evaluation of questionnaires and findings

1 As the graphs and figures indicate, the overall difference of opinion between boys and staff is quite large. The average difference is one mean raw score point or greater on the relationship dimensions of involvement, support, and on the treatment programmed dimension of autonomy.

2 To identify items on which staff and boys showed very large differences, I calculated the average proportion of true responses for each of the items separately for all the boys and staff in the normative sample.

3 In the March questionnaire and, to a certain extent in the November one (particularly in the comparative group), boys and staff showed differences of 25 per cent or greater on eight items. Some items which staff answered True at least more often than boys by as much as 25 per cent were: 'Staff go out of their way to help residents' and 'Staff set an example for neatness'. On the contrary, boys answered true 25 per cent plus more often than staff such items as: 'Staff are always changing their mind here' and 'There is very little group spirit in the house'.

4 There are three distinct findings:
  (a) The differing attitudes in the 'hard-core' house in March and November.
  (b) The similarity of attitudes in the comparison house in March and November.
  (c) The much closer liaison between staff and boys in the experimental 'hard-core' house in the second testing.

5 Looking at these three points in greater detail, let us compare the two results from Shackleton House as seen by the boys. There are some sweeping alterations, as much as plus two raw score points. In the March testing, eight or more boys answered 'True' to the following:

Staff have very little time to encourage boys. (80 per cent)
Boys rarely talk about their personal problems with other
  boys. (90 per cent)
The staff give the boys very little responsibility. (100 pcr cent)
All decisions about the house are made by the staff and not

CIES Figure 1

Raw score profiles of boys perception of the 'hard-core' house (Shackleton) in March and November 1975

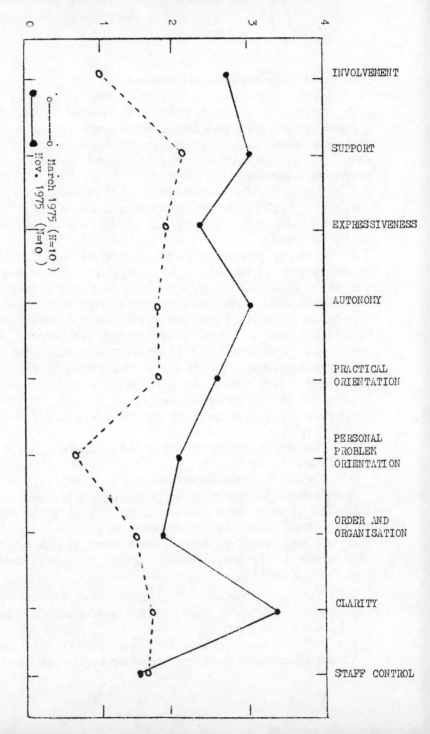

CIES Figure 2

Raw score profiles of staff perception of the 'hard-core' house (Shackleton) in March and November 1975

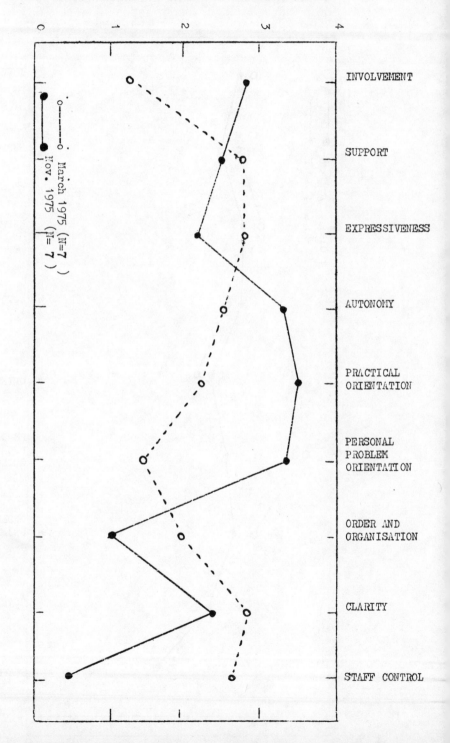

CIES Figure 3

Raw score profiles of boys perception of the comparison house (Nansen) in March and November 1975

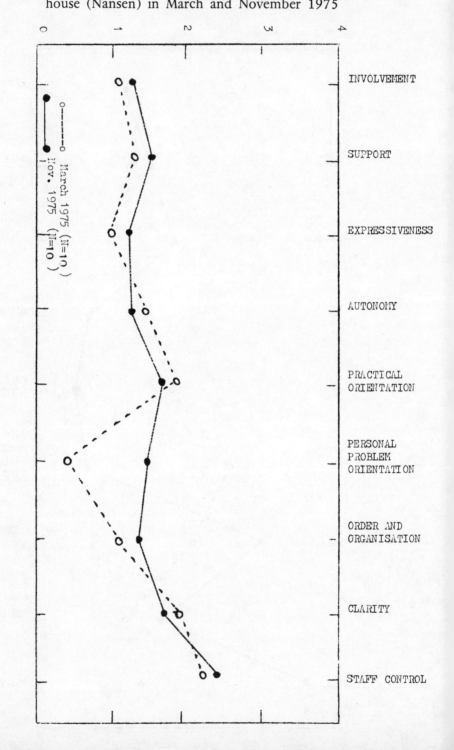

Raw score profiles of staff perception of the comparison
house (Nansen) in March and November 1975

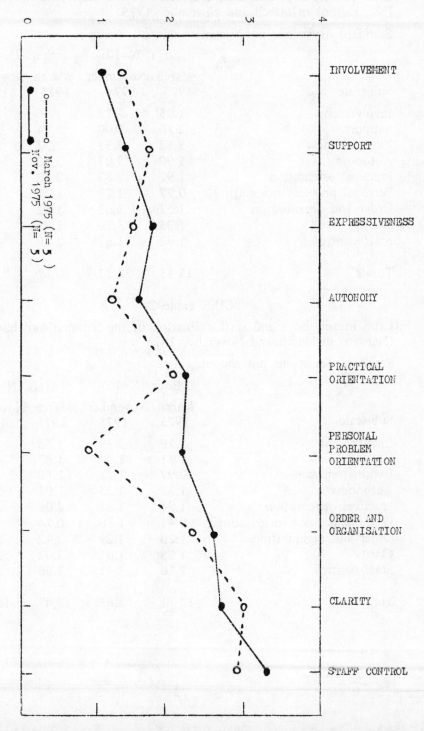

CIES Table 1

CIES means—boys and staff evaluation of the 'hard-core' house (Shackleton) in March and November 1975.

Standard deviations not shown.

Sub-scales	Boys (N=10)		Staff (N=7)	
	March 1975	November 1974	March 1975	November 1975
Involvement	1.05	2.72	1.46	2.93
Support	2.10	3.00	2.74	2.60
Expressiveness	2.12	2.51	2.72	2.00
Autonomy	1.90	3.05	2.50	3.24
Practical orientation	1.92	2.87	2.12	3.49
Personal problem orientation	0.77	1.79	1.21	3.31
Order and organisation	1.62	1.62	1.82	1.32
Clarity	1.93	3.20	2.91	2.40
Staff control	1.92	1.61	2.69	0.87
Totals	15.33	22.37	20.17	22.16

CIES Table 2

CIES means—boys and staff evaluation of the 'comparison' house (Nansen) in March and November 1975.

Standard deviations not shown.

Sub-scales	Boys (N=10)		Staff (N=5)	
	March 1975	November 1975	March 1975	November 1975
Involvement	1.29	1.39	1.35	1.11
Support	1.51	1.80	1.87	1.63
Expressiveness	0.97	1.21	1.60	1.82
Autonomy	1.32	1.23	1.03	1.22
Practical oritentation	1.93	1.61	2.08	2.30
Personal problem orientation	0.41	1.30	0.74	2.16
Order and organisation	1.20	1.29	2.42	2.61
Clarity	1.98	1.61	3.02	2.50
Staff control	2.10	2.41	2.96	3.17
Totals	12.71	13.85	17.07	18.52

by the boys. (80 per cent)
Staff are always changing their mind here. (80 per cent)

Similarly, eight or more boys answered 'False' to the following:

The staff act on boys' suggestions. (90 per cent)
If a boy's programme or timetable is changed, someone on
  the staff tells him why. (100 per cent)
Boys are encouraged to show their feelings. (90 per cent)
Boys are proud of their house. (90 per cent)
Personal problems are openly talked about. (100 per cent)
Boys may criticise staff members to their face. (100 per cent)
People say what they really think around here. (90 per cent)
Boys in this house care about each other. (80 per cent)
Boys have a say about what goes on here. (80 per cent)

6 In the November testing in Shackleton, the difference in stated
attitudes was considerable. Shown as 'True' this time:

Staff have very little time to encourage boys. (20 per cent)
Boys rarely talk about their personal problems with other
  boys. (20 per cent)
The staff give the boys very little responsibility. (40 per cent)
All decisions about the house are made by the staff and not
  by the boys. (0)
100 per cent stated that this was 'False' as compared to 80
  per cent who stated it to be 'True' in March.
Staff are always changing their minds here. (40 per cent)

Shown as 'False' this time:

The staff act on boys' suggestions. (30 per cent)
If a boy's programme or timetable is changed, someone on the
  staff tells him why. (20 per cent)
A significant alteration in boy/staff communication.
Boys are encouraged to show their feelings. (50 per cent)
Boys are proud of their house. (20 per cent)
Personal problems are openly talked about. (50 per cent)
Boys may criticise staff members to their face. (40 per cent)
People say what they really think around here. (30 per cent)
Boys in this house care about each other. (50 per cent)
Boys have a say about what goes on here. (20 per cent)

7 It is obvious, at a glance, that there appears to have been a
radical change in boy/boy and boy/staff relationships in Shackleton between the tests. I felt that this was because of the experiment, but decided to carry out more tests and observations
before feeling confident enough to claim that the experiment was
a success.

8 With the boys in Nansen House, used as a comparison group, there was a much less marked change in the results, the only significant one being in personal problem orientation. There did seem to be a slightly more cohesive spirit of boys assisting each other. This may have been in some way influenced by the fact that the senior staff member of the house changed during the gap between these tests.

If there had been marked and drastic changes in Nansen between the two tests, it could have meant that the drastic changes in Shackleton were caused by events other than the experimental scheme.

Other than the fact that the staff in Nansen also thought that there had been a much better relationship between the boys and their attitudes towards each other, there was no really significant change in staff answers in Nansen for the two tests.

9 Perhaps one of the most significant factors was the different attitudes of staff in Shackleton House between March and November, especially in the fact that they felt, in the later testing, much less need to use formal controls as is shown in the difference of 1.82 raw score points.

As with the boys, I decided to analyse some of their findings in March and compare them with the later findings in November. Once again, I decided to only use those points where, in the March tests, staff had shown an 80 per cent plus on 'False' or 'True'. To maintain similarities with the boys' results, I show as percentages rounded up or down to the 10 per cent scale.

10 Staff statements. The first figure shows the March result: the second the November result.

Items in which Shackleton staff showed, by at least 80 per cent as being 'True' in the March testing:

> There is very little emphasis in making plans for leaving Ardale. (80 per cent and 20 per cent)
> Boys tend to hide their feelings from the staff. (90 per cent and 10 per cent)

Items in which Shackleton staff showed, by at least 80 per cent as being 'False' in the March testing:

> Boys are expected to share their personal problems with each other. (80 per cent and 20 per cent)
> The staff help new boys get acquainted with the house. (80 per cent and 20 per cent)
> Staff sometimes argue with each other. (80 per cent and 40 per cent)
> At least they felt in the second testing that they could be

more honest in answering this question. The boys showed it as 50 per cent in both the March and November tests.

Boys are encouraged to plan for the future. (90 per cent and 20 per cent)

Personal problems are openly talked about. (100 per cent and 40 per cent)

This is a very well organised house. (80 per cent and 10 per cent)

Boys have a say about what goes on here (80 per cent and 10 per cent)

Summary

Having carried out the testing in as professional and impartial a method as possible, I felt that the results as shown had some validity. Obviously, it would be foolish to state that this method proved conclusively that the new set up with the 'hard-core' boys was a total success, but it does quite clearly show that the experiment was having some impact on both the boys and staff in Shackleton. Other forms of testing and evaluation should be able to give further feedback on the validity of the above findings.

7 Evaluating behaviour modification

Behaviour modification refers to the use of environmental happenings and events in a planned and ordered fashion to attempt to alter a person's response to a given stimulus. I have previously discussed the various methods outlined to help the staff to think closely at what is, after all, one of the main functions of a CH(E)— to help alter the boys' general behaviour so that they are less likely to commit further crime when they leave.

To some extent, the reluctance of CH(E)s and their respective social service departments to develop behavioural techniques, many of which are common in the United States of America, is based on a lack of funds and resources in Great Britain. There is absolutely no doubt that the American equivalents to CH(E)s have developed behavioural techniques to a very sophisticated level. Funding, finance and staff training is far more advanced with our colleagues across the Atlantic.

There are one or two definite techniques to alter, measure and record changes of behaviour in a residential setting. For the sake of this work, we ignore all clinical and other methods which cannot be used in a CH(E).

The main methods which are acceptable, or reasonably acceptable, methods in a CH(E) are:

1 On-going recording of behaviour by staff.
2 Group work pressures on boys to moderate behaviour and recording of findings of key workers and, in some cases, the boys themselves.
3 Conditioning.
4 Interviews, including stress interviews.
5 Intensive counselling.
6 Token economy schemes.
7 Rewards and privileges schemes—with the necessary withdrawal of such.

Methods not used in the 'hard-core' experiment

Without the help of a trained psychologist, and having only the minimal use of a visiting consultant psychiatrist, I did not feel personally competent enough to organise an operative or respondant conditioning group. It was, of course, possible to carry out certain experiments for the sake of experimenting, but anything of this nature would be false and not permanent. For example, if the serving hatches from the kitchen to the dining room were slammed down and no more food served until the volume of noise in the dining room was at a certain level, meals would be much quieter. However, this form of conditioning would only last as long as the boy was at Ardale. Besides, most of the staff regard a certain amount of social interplay at meals to be a good thing.

Token economies are an established form of treatment with juvenile delinquents in the USA, but have not been widely used in this country. This scheme was ruled out because of the age of the boys, the lack of experience in running such a scheme, the extra problems envisaged with young and inexperienced staff, and a personal lack of conviction in the scheme in the mid-1970s.

The basis of such a scheme is that each boy is personally responsible for his own behaviour. The boys are able to earn tokens by achieving personalised behavioural targets. They are able to earn tokens for obtaining individual targets which are stated on target cards they carry around with them. Against each space on the card tokens are stuck on or stamped when a particular target has been reached. For example, a boy may get a token for waking and rising promptly, regularly saying 'please' and 'thank you' or good behaviour at meal times. The tokens can then be exchanged for rewards which may be sweets, extra television, a day trip home, etc. As will be seen shortly, Ardale's rewards and privileges scheme has many of the basics of a token economy scheme without the actual obtaining of tokens—with all the problems that entails of fraud, bullying and curruption. With the right number of competent and experienced staff, with the full support of each boy's social worker, it should be possible to organise a token economy scheme to help modify behaviour at Ardale. However, for the period the 'hard-core' experiment was in progress, this method was not used or even very seriously considered.

On-going evaluation of behaviour changes

Prior to a boy—every boy and not just the 'hard-core' group—arriving at Ardale, a file is formed, initially comprising of the report from the Regional Assessment Centre and copies of any letters sent to the social worker. The left hand inside cover contains a number of blank occurrence sheets. These are for all categories of staff to record any on-going occurrence which may be of benefit to other staff in helping a boy fulfill his treatment programme.

The main difficulty is, however, that only a minimal number of staff have daily access to the files without seeking a member of staff with a key to the office filing cabinets. Teachers, therefore, have much less access to a boy's file than do the housestaff. The second problem with occurrence sheets is that with the day to day pressures of solving problems, the actual recording of them becomes a chore which is often put off and sometimes ignored completely.

An argument frequently presented is that the information is confidential and once it appears on an occurrence sheet it is available for anybody to read. However, the most obvious drawback with occurrence sheets is the staff's natural proclivity to record only negative information. One is far more likely to read: 'Fred absconded again last night' than: 'Fred did very well in yesterday's football match and scored the winning goal'.

Having stressed the need for on-going assessment, and knowing the natural failings of occurrence sheets, it was felt necessary with the 'hard-core' group at least, to devise some more accurate means of recording and evaluating the staff's impression of boys' behaviour.

The Ardale 'hard-core rating of behaviour

1 A very simple rating scale of from zero to ten was created which would give even the most hurried member of staff, or reticent boy the simple chore of ringing a number he felt appropriate to behaviour at the time. All concerned knew the scale: O = terrible; 1 = very bad; 2 = bad; 3 = poor; 4 = below average; 5 = fair; 6 = average; 7 = above average; 8 = quite good; 9 = very good; 10 = excellent.

2 Also devised were some simple forms to fill in for both boys and staff which, not only incorporated the rating scales, but gave scope for added information.

3 Once again, borrowing from Moos, I devised three questionnaires based on the adjustment to residential milieu scale which would back up our own tests.

4 No boy or member of staff was forced to co-operate, although we did use group pressures on the boys who showed little interest. Some of the tests were for a period of three months only, some were on-going, and one was specifically geared to the beginning and end of stay at Ardale.

The CIES adjustment to residential milieu scale

Three basic findings were sought about a group of boys from the 'hard-core' group and a similar sample from the comparison group, i.e., behaviour with staff; behaviour with peers; behaviour in activities.

This specific test was given twice, in March and November 1975, using the same groups as in the social climate tests. All the staff concerned were given a written outline of how to carry out the recording and what we hoped to discover. This, simplified down to its essentials, stated:

1 *Behaviour with staff*

The rated boy's behaviour towards the adults responsible for his treatment within Ardale in general but ..... House in particular.

2 *Behaviour with peers*

The rated boy's behaviour towards the other boys living with him at Ardale in general but in ..... House in particular.*

3 *Behaviour in activities*

The rated boy's behaviour in activities where he has to learn a skill or a behaviour to produce something (e.g., school work, workshop, sport, etc.).

*Shackleton (hard-core) or Nansen (comparison).

Evaluation of the findings of the two questionnaires on behaviour as per the residential milieu scale

1 To keep in line with later testing, we used a ten point scale even with only five questions on each of the three questionnaires. Two corresponds to the non-co-operative boy with ten being the extremely co-operative lad. It is worthy of note that no single member of staff rated a ten with any of the 'hard-core' group and only three tens were rated with the comparison group—all of them on the questionnaire on behaviour in activities.
2 The results would appear to indicate two salient facts:
(a) the overall improvement in behaviour;
(b) the very positive increase in behaviour with the 'hard-core' group.

Obviously with such small samples as this, it would be a dangerous generalisation to state that CH(E)s have a positive influence on the behaviour of the boys resident within them. However, the results certainly indicate that, with the samples used, there was a definite improvement in behaviour.
3 Staff felt that eight boys from the 'hard-core' group had improved

Figure 7.1
Mean average ratings* of the results of the residential milieu questionnaire replies
The 'hard-core' group

Boys	Behaviour Staff		Behaviour Peers		Behaviour in activities	
	March 1975	November 1975	March 1975	November 1975	March 1975	November 1975
1	2	6	2	8	2	8
2	2	6	2	6	2	6
3	2	4	2	6	4	8
4	4	8	2	4	4	6
5	4	6	4	8	4	6
6	4	6	4	8	6	8
7	4	6	4	6	6	6
8	4	4	4	4	6	6
9	4	4	6	8	6	6
10	6	8	6	6	8	8
Totals	36	58	36	64	48	68

Figure 7.2
The comparison group

Boys	Behaviour Staff		Behaviour Peers		Behaviour in activities	
	March 1975	November 1975	March 1975	November 1975	March 1975	November 1975
1	2	4	2	4	2	4
2	4	6	2	4	2	4
3	4	4	4	4	2	6
4	4	4	4	4	4	4
5	6	6	4	4	4	6
6	6	6	4	6	4	6
7	6	6	4	6	6	6
8	6	6	6	6	6	8
9	6	6	6	6	8	8
10	8	6	6	8	8	8
Totals	52	54	42	52	46	60

*Rounded up or down to the nearest whole figure.

their behaviour with staff, with two boys remaining unchanged and no boys deteriorating.

4 Staff felt that only two boys from the comparison group had improved their behaviour with staff, with seven remaining unchanged and one actually deteriorating—this boy, however, had the highest rating of all (8) for behaviour with staff in the March questionnaire.

5 The results were similar with the 'hard-core' group in relation to peer group behaviour; eight improving, a few drastically, and two remaining static.

6 With the comparison group for relationships with peers, staff felt that five had improved and five remained unchanged.

7 Staff felt that the 'hard-core' group's behaviour in activities had improved six times and remained unchanged four times. However, the four that remained unchanged had scored quite highly in the March test.

8 The results were similar with the comparison group's behaviour in activities. Six improved and four remained unchanged.

9 Taking the rounded up totals, it was seen that the staff evaluation of ratings of improvement were:

Behaviour with staff	H-C Group 22	Comp.Group	2
Behaviour with peers	H-C Group 28	Comp.Group	10
Behaviour—activities	H-C Group 20	Comp.Group	14

10 Therefore, according to the staff evaluation, using the three questionnaire results only, the general behaviour of the 'hard-core' group increased by seventy rated points, while that of the comparative group increased by twenty-six.

Summary

As stated earlier, the samples were too small to really prove or disprove anything except to evaluate a small experiment in one particular CH(E). The results as they stood meant very little regarding a positive increase in behaviour. However, taken with the other findings based on the behavioural modification techniques being used (see following pages) there was definitely some feeling that Ardale was working towards a positive goal.

On-going evaluation of boys' behaviour by staff

In February 1975, approximately six months after the first 'hard-core' boy had been admitted to the two month trial experiment, I at last got around tó supplementing the scanty information on occurrence sheets by devising a small questionnaire for staff to complete at regular intervals on each boy. This included the simple rating scale. It was initially intended to ask the staff directly concerned with the experiment and the comparison group to administer this questionnaire to themselves weekly. However, it was soon found that it was more convenient to have it done monthly. The questionnaire is shown in Figure 7.3.

Figure 7.3

The questionnaire

Staff evaluation of behaviour of ....
for month ending ....

Name of Staff ....   Post held ....

1 Comments on general behaviour

2 Why do you think his
  behaviour is better or
  worse than in your
  last report?

3 Rating scale

Please circle one only even if you have made no comments above.

O terrible; 1 very bad; 2 bad; 3 poor; 4 below average; 5 fair;
6 average; 7 above average; 8 quite good; 9 very good; 10 excellent.

4 Anything extra
  you wish to add.

Confidential

Sampling technique

After only a relatively short period, I began to become inundated with information and soon realised that I would not be able to fully record and analyse all the information coming in.

It was decided to use four sample groups of ten boys each, chosen completely at random. Ten boys were taken from the 'hard-core' house, and ten from the comparison house in April 1975. Six months later, in November 1975, another ten boys from each of the two houses were used. In each case I recorded, charted and graphed their progress and/or regression for six consecutive months and was then

82

able to compare the alteration in behaviour of the two groups on two separate occasions.

As will be shown shortly, we did record briefly the results of every one of the 'hard-core' group, whether or not he was in one of the sampling groups. By so doing, we were later able to compare the staff evaluation of a boy's behaviour one month after he arrived and a month before he left. This was found to be very useful, especially when linked with the boys' own evaluation of their own behaviour.

Although in our evaluation, we draw conclusions from the various findings, only one typical graph is given here. In all cases we have identified the boy by a number only, in the interests of confidentiality. These results are shown in Figure 7.4.

Evaluation of the on-going method of assessment of behaviour

1 Like any similar scheme, it was obvious that the actual recording could be affected by any number of variables: staff disinterest, something to be rushed once a month, a boy who had been doing well but on the day of the recording had annoyed the member of staff or, vice versa, a boy who had been a perpetual nuisance but on the day of the recording had made some special effort, actual like or dislike of a particular boy, etc. However, it was felt that a fairly consistent rating probably indicated that the member of staff had been as impartial as he or she could be. On a pure statistical basis, the method had too many flaws in to indicate anything on its own. Linked, however, with other tests and questionnaires on behaviour, the results seemed promising.

2 There was a considerable accumulation of material to sort out and record. This should be taken into account by anyone wishing to conduct a similar experiment.

3 Gradually, as staff became aware that there was more interest in their numerical rating of a boy, they began to write less and less in the other three sections of the questionnaire. A few, however, regularly answered the section relating to improvement or deterioration in behaviour. As there were only four occasions when behaviour was shown to make a deterioration in a month (none from the 'hard-core' group) this gave some indication of whether or not staff felt that the behaviour modification techniques being used—group work, counselling, rewards and privileges scheme, interviews, etc.—were working. Some of the reasons given for why staff felt that behaviour had improved in the past month are:

He is at last beginning to learn and obey the rules.

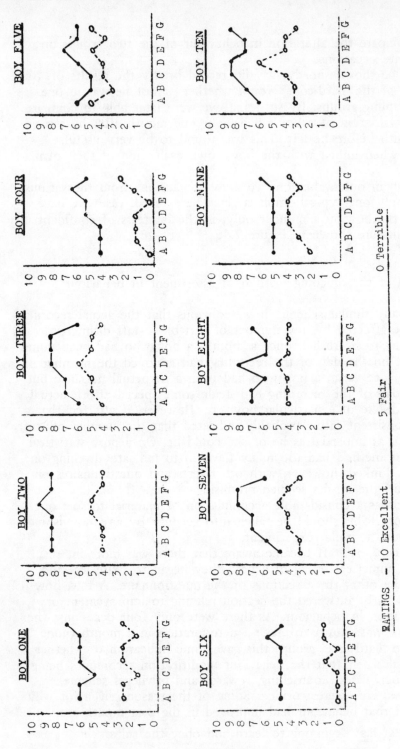

RATINGS — 10 Excellent   5 Fair   0 Terrible

A to G — members of House and teaching staff

November 1975 O-----O   April 1976 ●———●

Figure 7.4

The fear of losing his weekend leave again.

Because his mates have told him every body is laughing at him.

The influence of the group.

He says he will prove to every body he can get the early bus two weeks on the trot.

I feel that our counselling sessions are really beginning to influence his behaviour.

God only knows, but it is.

He knows he has a review this month.

The other lads in his group have made it clear that he is the group clown and he doesn't like it.

I don't think it's anything we do; he's just a month older and perhaps a month wiser.

It could be because of group pressures, but I'm not sure.

He's after a single room.

His girlfriend visiting really helps.

There has been a reconcilliation between him and his parents.

He says only the good lads get the cushy paid jobs like cleaning the principal's car.

He's at last beginning to think of the future.

4 Many more could be cited, some very serious, some amusing and some downright derogatory. One of my favourites is: He knows that every body expects him to continue his stupid pattern of behaviour so he is making a great show of improving just to put two fingers up to us all and say 'See you bastards, I proved you wrong!'

5 The rating scales for the first 'hard-core' groups showed an average improvement of between three and four places. The biggest improvements a boy from this group made was seven rating points from a one in April to an eight in September. Only seven boys were rated by any of the staff members as making no real improvement during the period and no boys were shown as regressing.

6 The second 'hard-core' group showed similar improvements, with the average being, once again between three and four places. Only two boys were rated as not making any improvement and none were shown as regressing. Although mainly different boys were used to the residential milieu rating scale questionnaires, it is interesting to note that the end results were very similar.

7 The two comparison groups also made a marked improvement in

behaviour, but the average was less—two to three points in the first testing and only two points in the second series. The highest recorded jump any boy made was five points. There were far more boys shown as making no progress and four were shown as regressing (two from each of the sample groups).

8 To summarise: the general results indicated a link up with the earlier findings. It began to appear that the experimental scheme with the 'hard-core' boys was having some marked success in improving general behaviour within the school but could it be maintained? Only follow-up results would indicate that.

The experimental rewards and privileges scheme

Group work with teenage delinquents is a laborious and often heart breaking job with too much overt testing-out and very rarely any quick or spectacular results.

It was obvious that we would have to adapt what can only be called standard group work to something more applicable to some of the most difficult, delinquent and often dangerous youngsters in the country. After various discussions we decided to use a rewards and privileges scheme backed up by a withdrawal of these rewards and privileges and a sanctions scheme. We were aware of some—but not all—of the difficulties and how the system could be open to abuse. I read considerably of the many similar schemes run in American correctional homes for young delinquents and realised that I would not have the same support as my American counterparts.

In the end it was decided that the majority of the sanctions to be used would be a withdrawal of privileges and perhaps a few things boys expected as their rights as well. I would not use corporal punishment, had no facility to use temporary isolation, and was not allowed by the Community Home Regulations to use deprivation of food. Gradually a list of rewards and sanctions was drawn up and then came the problem of what to administer them for and how to allocate them fairly.

The rewards	The sanctions
In increasing order of value	*In increasing order of importance*
Extra cigarettes or sweets	No visits to village shop
Escorted cinema trip	No cinema trip
Stay up for late TV	No late TV
Paid job in spare time	Extra schoolwork in spare time
Extra pocket money	Fine
A single bedroom	Confined to school grounds

86

The rewards	The sanctions
Radio after lights out	No snooker or dart playing
Unescorted cinema, disco or youth club visit	No swimming or ball games
Day pass in mid-week	No weekend day pass
Early weekend leave (from Friday lunchtime)	Late weekend leave (held back until Saturday)
Extra weekend leave (Monday)	Weekend leave cancelled
Girlfriend can visit in evenings or weekends	Part of main leave periods cut or reduced.

How the rewards could be earned

General politeness to staff—use of 'please' and 'thank you'.
Politeness to each other.
Getting up when told and making bed properly.
Good behaviour in dining room.
Care of house property—snooker tables, dart boards, etc.
Good reports from schoolrooms and workshops.
Volunteering for unpaid jobs, e.g. sweeping out TV room.
Involvement in group work.
Good reports from parents about weekends spent at home.
Special recommendations from key workers.
Special acts of kindness to peers.
Trying to prevent other boys absconding or misbehaving.
General improvement in behaviour reported by all members of staff concerned with the house.

Reasons for sanctions being imposed

A Minor

Continual swearing after being warned, especially in presence of female staff or visitors.
General horseplay, e.g. throwing food around in dining room.
Smoking in unauthorised areas, e.g. in bedrooms.

B Intermediate

Being missing from lessons without permission.
Absconding.
Going to village shop without permission.
Challenging staff.
Constant agitation.
Failing to comply with rules or orders.

Refusal to carry out a command given by a member of staff.

C *Major*

Vandalism and destruction of property.
Physical or intense verbal aggression.
Stealing (or receiving or possessing stolen goods).
Sexual bullying or intimidation.
Extortion, pressure and bullying.
Possession of a weapon.
Threatening another person or persons with a weapon.

Assessing behaviour and awarding rewards or sanctions

It was obvious that the boys should initially know what the various standards of behaviour were we expected at Ardale and what could be earned or lost by observing or not observing these standards or rules. It was the job of every boy's key worker to bring these to light initially, although many of the group meetings were to discuss behaviour. It was felt that the frequent discussion of good and bad behaviour was, in itself, a relevant value in modifying it.

We operated a system for a few weeks of holding court with the boys to discuss each member's behaviour and who should be rewarded and punished and what the rewards and punishments should be. This was our first mistake. The boys were far more inclined to be over punitive with each other and, whereas we only intended a sanction to last for one, two, or at the most three weeks, the boys were suggesting that their peers should be fined all their pocket money or not allowed to the cinema for six months or stopped weekend leave for weeks on end. Even close friends were hard on each other if they felt that they were letting down the side or the house.

After three or four weeks of trying to get the boys to be less punitive towards each other, it was decided to take the matter of rewards and sanctions out of their hands. A group was formed consisting of the two deputy principals and the senior housestaff to decide who should be rewarded or who deprived of certain privileges. This regular group became known as the deputy principals' meeting. Whatever acts had been carried out, both negative and positive, this tribunal was able to see that the rewards and sanctions were fairly awarded.

Various changes have been made over the last few years, but, during the time of the 'hard-core' experiment, the weekly tribunal did, in itself, contribute something towards modifying behaviour.

1 For the period from January to December 1975, nineteen new 'hard-core' boys were admitted to the group already formed.
Eleven of the group left during the period.
2 The average number of 'hard-core' boys during any month was twenty-two.
3 In one average month (June 1975) the boys in the 'hard-core' group were awarded a total of sixty-one rewards, and twenty-three sanctions.
4 The most common reward was early or extra weekend leave (537 times given to the 'hard-core' group in 1975) and the most common sanctions were fines (124) and late weekend leave (136).
5 Only one of the 'hard-core' group used a weapon on another boy (stabbing) and seven knives, one air rifle and two air pistols were confiscated. The police were called in for the stabbing and the boy eventually went to Borstal.
6 Fines ranged from ten to fifty pence and the money received was placed in the Boys Fund and used to help pay for the rewards of extra cash, cigarettes, sweets, etc. In effect, the boys with a positive behaviour improvement were partly financed by the boys with a negative behaviour rating.
7 Of the nineteen new boys admitted in the year, only two never received some sanction and all nineteen received some reward at least twice during the year.
8 We all felt that the system worked and would have liked to elaborate upon it. One of the reasons we ceased using it as such was the visiting auditors stated that if we fined boys the money must go back to the local authority and not be used to further finance the behaviour modification scheme.

The boys evaluation of their own behaviour

Most of this section has been devoted to describing a few methods used to help modify behaviour and various evaluation techniques carried out by the staff. There was one other evaluatory method used and one which caused some worry amongst the staff because it was completely confidential to me and the 'hard-core' boys. This method was not used with the comparative groups.

I personally interviewed every single one of the 'hard-core' group on at least four occasions provided they stayed here the full period and did not leave because they had committed some further offence and were sent to pastures new. Most of the interviewing was done on an informal basis, in the boy's own room or while walking around the school grounds. However, the first interview, approximately four weeks after a boy's arrival and the final interview, approximately four weeks before we had agreed a boy could leave, were held in my office. I explained that I was seeking information in absolute confidence, and asked the boy to fill in the questionnaire, shown in figure 7.5. This was always done in my office at the time of the interview, and I honoured my promise of confidentiality.

Figure 7.5

The questionnaire to the boys

I want you to fill this in for me today so that I personally know how I can help make things better in Ardale. I give you my firm promise that whatever you write will not be shown to or discussed with *any* boy nor *any* member of staff.

1 What do you really think of your house?
2 Which member of your group of staff (including the teachers who work in your house) do you get on best with. Why?
3 Which of your staff group do you not get on with. Why?
4 What do you think should be done to improve the general standard of behaviour in the house?
5 Do you think you will get into more trouble when you leave Ardale. Why?
6 Below is a list from zero to ten. It is about your *behaviour* only. You tell me where you think you fit in by circling the most appropriate number.

0 terrible; 1 very bad; 2 bad; 3 poor; 4 below average; 5 fair; 6 average; 7 above average; 8 quite good; 9 very good; 10 excellent.

Thank you. You can write your name here if you want, but it does not matter if you do not wish to.

Evaluating the 'hard-core' boys' questionnaires on behaviour

1 The most obvious feature was the estimated similarity of behaviour improvement between the boys and staff results.
2 In not one single case did the boys estimate a regression or halt in behaviour improvement during the time in the experiment at Ardale.
3 In some cases, the individual boy estimated that his behaviour had improved by five or six rated points, although the average was between two and three.
4 The average rating for the first test came between poor and

90

fair, but in the latter testing recorded, a rating of between average and quite good. It is significant that in the first testing no boy rated himself as terrible and only one as very bad. In the latter testing no boy rated himself very good or excellent.

5 In the initial test results, the most popular member of staff was the housewarden but, in the second test, this was more spread out and he, one teacher and a housemother took about equal points.

6 The most disliked person was a teacher on both the questionnaires.

7 The standard answer to question 1 was 'alright' in the first testing to 'it's a good house' in the latter test. There were some deviations from this, many quite amusing (e.g. 'it's a cross between a workhouse and a doss house'), but over 80 per cent recorded answers similar to stated above.

8 A number of boys left question 4 blank in the first testing, but only four did so in the latter tests. The punitive aspect was paramount. In the second tests, no less than eleven boys made reference to the cane—which has never been used during my tenure at Ardale.

9 There were however, some positive replies based on an increase in group work and counselling. A basic token economy scheme was suggested by one boy: 'All boys should have a book with them in which the staff write down if they have been better or worse each day'.

10 Of the fifty boys who took the test initially, twenty-two left question five blank, eighteen indicated they did not know, three said they would not get into further trouble and five indicated that it was more than likely. In the latter test (forty-four boys), although two still indicated that they probably would get into more trouble and sixteen were not sure, twenty-six indicated that they felt they had a good chance of keeping out of further trouble. I knew that only follow-up results would indicate how accurate their prophesies were.

8 Educational evaluation of the 'hard-core' group

I have described earlier the background work carried out in preparing two specific teachers and groups of boys for a programme of educational modification (see p.44 ff). It was necessary to let all concerned be aware of the needs to run small classes (or groups) outside the normal schoolroom atmosphere. Some of the groups were still held in the general education block, but now in relaxed and informal settings. The library was modernised and made into an educational resources room where many boys went, initially to do as little as possible, but were soon producing work at their own level and speed which, on many occasions, far outstripped the conventional classrooms. The methods outlined earlier were put into practice and, in the main, had a high level of success.

The standard in the workshops was, right from the start, geared to the individual just as much as the more academic lessons. Boys were expected to enjoy what they were doing but this would never be possible if all the boys were forced to make the same things at the same time. Much of the work of certain departments was not related to personal production of goods to take home but the element of pride of work was installed as soon as possible. The boys in the building department were frequently praised by visitors to the school for their work in renovating the swimming pool and the various walls they built around areas of ornamental rockery. The motor mechanics department serviced the two school mini-buses and the element of friendly rivalry between the groups working on each vehicle was encouraged.

We began to do a lot of work for the local community in the workshops—repairing broken bikes for a children's home, mending toys at a local hospital being but two. The lads began to see that there were people who actually had more problems than they themselves.

As one of our hypotheses was that the experiment should show an alteration in the educational progress of the 'hard-core' group, much of the rest of this section now deals with facts and statistics to prove or disprove that suggestion.

Reading ability

The majority of boys coming into Ardale, having passed through a Regional Assessment Centre, had been given various tests in reading and reading comprehension which culminated in a Reading Age Score (RA).

Tests differ slightly at the various RACs, but two fairly standard ones are still Burt's reading test No.1 and Schonell's silent reading test B. The former is a graded vocabulary test which, to quote the author, 'is suitable for any child who has learnt to read; and, being both quick to administer and most suggestive in its implications, forms by far the best point at which to begin the general testing'. It considers 110 words in increasing order of difficulty and its range is from four to fifteen years. From this a fairly accurate reading age can be ascertained.

The Schonell silent reading test is one which examines a child's ability to understand the printed word. It consists of a number of prose paragraphs of increasing difficulty, from which key words have been omitted at intervals. The reader has to choose the correct word from five given words. The chance of a correct choice being obtained by guessing is, thus, one in five and the finished script of a reader who guesses as distinct from a poor reader is easily recognisable by an experienced tester. Its range is from 7.0 to 13.9 years. Any child completing this test accurately is shown as having a Reading Age (RA) of 13.9 plus years.

The problem with any form of reading test is that it very rarely copes with the child of super reading ability. Taking another test frequently used, the Schonell graded reading vocabulary test, no person—child or adult—completing the test absolutely accurately can show a RA of more than fifteen plus years. To obtain this score, the child (or adult) must be able to correctly pronounce (but not necessarily understand the meaning of) words such as: ineradicable; judicature; preferential; homonym; fictitious; rescind; metamorphosis; somnambulist; bibliography; idiosyncrasy.

Whatever the actual tests used, it is a well known fact that reading ages (and reading comprehension ages) are, with many delinquent children, greatly retarded when compared with actual chronological ages, although this is frequently not linked to a low IQ. A child individually reading to his teacher daily is still one of the best methods of encouraging reading. To me, every teacher is a teacher of reading.

When I started the 'hard-core' experiment, Ardale had just appointed its first remedial subjects teacher. This in itself was thought to be a waste of a teacher by some staff in view of the fact that Ardale boys were supposed to be of at least average intelligence. It was a pre-supposed fact that the boys coming into Ardale were, at least, average readers. The information shown on the RAC reports that at least 25 per cent, and usually a lot more, had reading ages well below chronological age was sometimes not noticed or totally ignored. In 1973, boys were expected to be able to read and understand the various text books thrust under their noses: those that couldn't were regarded as being either bolshy or under-functioning, whatever that was supposed to mean.

From the start the Remedial Teacher concentrated on basic English and reading. As usual, I had no extra money to begin with so had to concentrate on individual work rather than the use of expensive teaching machines. I did manage to find a couple of old typewriters for the boys to use and gave this group the sole use of the school tape recorder.

In 1942, Dr Schonell wrote: 'Results of remedial measures reveal that what the backward reader requires most is a measure of individual attention. Often he has been the victim of class instruction and of unsuitable methods ...' (Schonell, 1942)

Dr Schonell goes on to say:

> He has limped along at the end of a group of children, most of whom were succeeding tolerably well; he has cried out for individual consideration of his difficulties, but in many instances, his cry has gone unsatisfied ...

This then, was one of the first major changes made. With boys in the remedial group, all work must be individual. It is perhaps worth noting at this stage that, because the group concentrated on English and to avoid the use of such terms as remedial, backward or slow-learning, we always referred to it as English Two, as different from English One which was mainly an examination group. It was feared that this group would be regarded by the lads as the 'dummy's' group and that no boy would wish to be associated with it: as it transpired, just the opposite happened, and there were a number of quite good readers who wanted to join.

One of the problems in relating reading and the comprehension of reading to boys over the age of thirteen is the sad lack of suitable reading material. A boy completely alone with his teacher may be prepared to read aloud 'Dick plays with Dora and takes Nip for a walk', but he is very rarely willing to do so in the immediate hearing of his peers. We did manage to find a few specially written books for older backward readers but, in the main they were written for middle class children and never seemed to take into account the different ethnic groups.

This has changed over the past few years. Using my experience with ESN boys, we made a series of graded cards, particularly relevant to our boys. We hunted for pictures and drawings of subjects interesting to thirteen to seventeen year old boys, stuck them on to cards, wrote a few simple words about them beneath each picture and, on the reverse, asked a few simple questions.

Most people, apart from those studying for examinations, read for pleasure. We knew that if we were going to get the boys interested in reading, we should choose subjects of general interest to their age range—football, violence, sex, cars, motorcycles, pop-idols, TV stars, being but a few. A typical example of a reading comprehension card showed a colour photo of a stock car race. Written underneath was:

> This is a stock car race. We can see nine cars. Two of them
> have crashed. The blue one has crashed into the yellow one.
> You can see the driver of the yellow car. He is not pleased.
> The red and white car may win the race. Have you ever
> been to a stock car race and seen cars crash into each other?

Note the repetition of the more difficult words yellow and crashed. On the reverse of the card would be a few simple questions which could be either answered orally to the teacher or, later done as a written exercise:

1 How many cars can you see?
2 Which cars have crashed?
3 Who is not pleased?
4 Which car will win?
5 Why do you think it will win?
6 Tell me about a stock car race you have seen or one you would like to go to.

Obviously, the cards were graded, getting progressively more difficult until the boy himself usually decided he wished to move from cards to text books. By this method, basic reading methods were linked with simple comprehension. All boys were encouraged initially to ask if they did not understand a particular word, but gradually they were taught to use a simple dictionary, which was always available on the teacher's desk, to look up words themselves. It came as quite a surprise to find that so few boys had ever used a dictionary and even less had been taught how to use one. A little bit of checking with the boys came up with the following rather disturbing results:

	Groups %		
	A	B	C
Boys never seen a dictionary	60	52	56
Boys never used a dictionary	82	74	74
Boys never shown how to use one	100	100	100

The above figures only reflect what the boys stated and may not be completely accurate. It was significant that the majority (over 80 per cent) of the boys who answered that they had used dictionaries, had spent some time in special residential schools prior to coming to Ardale.

With all groups, we carried out three specific tests to evaluate individual reading progress. This was all based on the Schonell graded reading test and was given at the beginning, after two months and at the end of each boy's stay. There was not one single boy who did not make some form of progress in his basic reading age, apart from the few boys who remained at Ardale for less than two months. It may be argued that reading age increases as does chronological age: this may be true for a child up to the age of about ten years, but the argument does not hold water with boys of fifteen plus who have convinced themselves they will never read, or been convinced by others that they are thick. The only successful answer is great patience and, by making reading matter interesting and relevant, convincing each individual boy that learning to read is not really a difficult process and is certainly worth while. Lessons on filling in forms, football coupons, applications for jobs, love letters, etc., all added to increasing a desire to catch up on lost time. See Table 8.1 for statistical results.

Table 8.1

Reading improvement with the 'hard-core' group

%

	RAC Finding	Admission Test	Leaving Test
RA above CA	32	38	44
RA commensurate to CA	28	36	42
RA below CA	18	26	6
RA not known	22	0	8*

*Boys who left before final test given.

Conclusions on reading improvement evaluation

Like any educational system, we did not obtain complete success, but a 20 per cent increase in boys who caught up to their chronological age in reading ability was mainly attributable to the concentrated effort in really trying to help boys with their reading problems. There is no simple cut and dried method I can advocate other than intense individual help, great patience, and, perhaps more important than anything, a considerable effort to make reading interesting to adolescent boys. If the teacher has poor relationships with the boys in his or her class, there will be little knowledge of what really interests the pupils.

Arithmetic ability

In 1973/74, Ardale was steeped in the tradition of being an ex-approved grammar school. Boys with an ability or an interest in maths were taught in a very similar fashion to the way I had been taught a quarter of a century earlier. There was no real policy for teaching remedial mathematics: every thing was geared to the number of examination passes.

The maths teacher was aware of the numbers of boys he had pushed to one side because the system in operation had not allowed him to devote time to any but those likely to reflect credit on the school by examination passes. The only other person who seemed really keen on making sums interesting was my deputy who, for years, had taught maths to approved school boys. Between the three of us, we devised various programmes for helping boys with arithmetic. Obviously, we still ran our examination groups and one or two of the 'hard-core' boys did exceptionally well in CSE and GCE passes.

It was decided that, with the majority of boys, the only success they were likely to have in improving basic mathematical concepts was to make the subject as interesting as possible and related to workshop techniques.

Numerous experiments were carried out to make maths interesting; entering the Daily Mail Bridge Competition, crosswords, football pools, the collation of vital statistics of peers, staff and girl friends being but a few. The introduction of decimal currency just a few years earlier complicated the teaching of a few who had no concept of currency, but the use of tens and hundreds gradually became much clearer. The fact that the boys received pocket money and handled their own cash helped, and many boys even kept their own accounts.

By far the most positive tool was the linking of classroom maths to workshop techniques. For example, the boys who spent most of their time in the building department, would have their maths related to building. Towards the end, a few boys could read a building blue-pring quite expertly. The motor mechanics department would have their maths geared to engine ratios and other technical matters.

Gradually, maths ceased to be the formidable ogre of the past with most—but not all—boys. The more interesting it became, the more the boys put into it and the more they got out of it. As with reading, we carried out our own testing, using the Staffordshire test of computation and the National Foundation Educational Research Mathematics Attainment Test B. Towards the middle of the 'hard-core' experiment, we were using a test which had been devised by ourselves. Table 8.2 shows the improvement achieved.

Table 8.2

Arithmetical improvement with the 'hard-core' group

	RAC Finding	Admission Test	Leaving Test
		%	
AA above CA	4	6	14
AA commensurate to CA	18	24	40
AA below CA	52	70	38
AA not known	26	0	8*

*Boys who left before final test administered.

Conclusions on arithmetic evaluation

Although some considerable improvement was shown, it is nowhere near as obvious as with the reading improvement. Perhaps mathematics is harder to teach than reading or perhaps we were getting our boys too late in their lives to do anything but scratch the surface of fifteen years mathematical retardation.

Perhaps my main consolation is that our figures, and hence our mathematical teaching methods, were considerably better than those produced by the Dartington Research Team into approved schools (1967-70). This team stated that in senior approved schools (which Ardale once was) 44 per cent of the inmates are up to six years retarded and 76 per cent are over six years retarded in arithmetic attainment. By our new teaching methods, we at least helped eight of the 'hard-core' group to arithmetically catch up with their chronological age. Perhaps not a very startling success but certainly one which pleased the boys, their social workers, and my maths teacher.

Examination work

For many years, Ardale has been a registered examination centre for both GCE and CSE. There has never been any reason to alter this. Quite a number of the 'hard-core' group had the basic ability to sit and pass CSE and GCE O level. In both cases, time was our biggest enemy. Many more boys would have been able to pass examinations if it had been possible to keep them longer.

Naturally, English and maths were the most common subjects taken at external level, but we have managed to get boys through history, geography, physics, chemistry, social studies, biology, art, technical drawing and various craft subjects such as woodwork. Some boys have scraped through and some have received high grades.

There was no significant difference numerically in the numbers of examination successes by the 'hard-core' and the normal intakes. This is quite remarkable really as very few people, including the Regional Assessment Centres and the social workers imagined so many of the deemed social failures would not only want (or be persuaded) to sit examinations, but actually pass. As with the normal groups many did not wish or were not competent to take external examinations, but those that did performed no worse than their peers with a better prognosis (see Table 8.3).

Table 8.3

The 'hard-core' examination results

Number of boys in the group	50
Number who sat examinations for CSE	36
Numbers who sat examinations for GCE	12
Numbers who passed CSE English	19
Numbers who failed CSE English	4
Numbers who passed CSE maths	8
Numbers who failed CSE maths	8
Numbers who passed GCE English Language	4
Numbers who failed GCE English Language	5
Numbers who passed GCE maths	1
Numbers who failed GCE maths	4
Numbers who passed in other GCE subjects	6
Numbers who failed in other GCE subjects	8
Maximum no. of CSE subjects taken by one boy	5
Maximum no. of GCE subjects taken by one boy	3

The above results in Table 8.3 speak for themselves. Given the right atmosphere, the right teaching, and the right incentives, even deemed failures can pass examinations.

Evaluating the results of vocational training

Apart from the few boys who sat external examinations in such subjects as woodwork, it was much harder to evaluate the actual positive improvement in the workshops. The craft instructors could give indications of improvement or deterioration, but this was all too often coloured by behaviour. Many of the boys had undergone some basic craft assessment in their Regional Assessment Centre but, in the main, we found this to be pretty meaningless. There is a vast difference in a boy carrying out some fundamental mechanical test in a RAC workshop and a boy working to a standard capable of getting him employment when he leaves.

The actual testing of manual dexterity and theoretical knowledge should not have been difficult, but some of the instructors had very little idea how to set about it. In the end the maths teacher evaluated the latter and reports written by craft instructors for case reviews were used to evaluate the former. There was no significant difference in either when compared with the normal intake. If anything, the actual ability to correctly handle tools was slightly higher with the 'hard-core' group, although we have never been able to elucidate why this was.

The main evaluation of vocational ability was carried out by myself in group activities and after the boys had left Ardale. All those boys who indicated that, when they left Ardale, they wished to follow in the trade or in one of the trades they had been taught here were noted and this information kept in a special file on each boy. This was then compared with the actual job they obtained when they left or one that they changed to shortly after leaving the first job. In the main, a large number of the boys did not live up to the expectations of their own ability. This was partly due to disillusionment and partly due to the employment situation in such seasonal trades as building. Quite a number of boys obtained jobs as motor mechanics only to find that they were petrol pump attendants. Even those who were told that they would eventually graduate to the more mechanical side of a garage often were unable to see any relevance between what they had been taught at Ardale and what the world had to offer them. If anything, the 'hard-core' group had a very strong desire for instant gratification in everything they did and this was often their undoing when they sought employment. In retrospect, perhaps we taught them too well and raised their ambitions too high for what we should have known was to face them when they left.

Table 8.4

Evaluation of trade training and employment with 'hard-core' group

Boys who stated they intended to seek employment in a trade taught to them at Ardale	40
Boys who obtained such employment in their first or second job after leaving	26
Boys who remained in this type of employment for at least six months	14
Boys who remained in this type of employment for over a year	8

Although the statistics in Table 8.4 appear quite depressing, they were not greatly different from the other boys at Ardale. As will be mentioned later, some of the boys got into further trouble with the law and were sent to Borstal, while some found it a much easier life to live on the dole. At least 20 per cent of the boys managed to achieve their ambitions and, once again, we should remember that we are only talking about boys who were supposed to be deemed failures. The long term effect will probably never be known.

Conclusions on the education of the 'hard-core' group

Although a CH(E) is not now exclusively a school but rather a community home with education on the premises, it is still regarded primarily as an educational establishment by the boys within it, their social workers, and large numbers of staff who work with the boys, even residential staff with no teaching experience or qualifications. I am personally referred to more often as headmaster than I am as principal, and more mail comes addressed to Ardale School than does addressed to Ardale. The majority of the boys are in the classrooms or workshops for five and a half hours per day for five days per week. If anybody thinks that the educational aspect of a CH(E) is minimal they have probably never visited one.

The very first hypothesis in relation to the 'hard-core' group states that the experiment should show distinct alteration in the educational pattern of the boys concerned as compared with their previous case histories prior to admission to Ardale. Although nobody could claim a 100 per cent success, statistics show that there was a definite increase not only in educational ability but in general interest in education.

9   Rule breaking and further criminality within Ardale

Absconding

> In CH(E)s, absconding by a pupil leads to anxiety among
> staff as it threatens the containing functions of the home,
> chills the institutional climate and puts the absentee at
> risk. But little is known about the reasons for persistent
> absconding. (Milham et al, 1978)

Probably more has been written about absconding from approved
schools and CH(E)s than any other aspect of these establishments.
It can be an emotive subject and makes easy publicity in local
and national newspapers.

One of the categories for 'hard-core' nomenclature was persistent
absconding. This was frequently the reason this type of boy had been
refused admission at other CH(E)s. After all, none of us really want
to 'chill the institutional climate'. Some quite well meaning people
possibly think that absconding is an illness caught at a CH(E) or an
earlier residential establishment: they rarely relate it to day school
truanting or what is now known as school phobia. In 1974, S. F.
Johnson, the Principal Adviser for Wessex Children's Regional
Planning Committee carried out research on the relation between
truanting and later absconding. He reported in the Community Home
Schools Gazette, September 1976, that over a half of children going
through Observation and Assessment Centres during the period covered were involved in truanting at a reportable level. There was, he
also found, a tendency for the truants to be the absconders and also
to have problems of aggression and violence.

Previous experience with many of the 'hard-core' boys follows a
very similar pattern to the above. The evidence tends to suggest
that truanting often leads to absconding and the pattern develops
over the years with some boys to a persistent level and they could
even be claimed as habitual absconders.

It was obvious from the onset of the 'hard-core' experiment that
it could possibly cut down further criminality if we could cut down
on absconding. Between 1969 and 1973, the Dartington Research
Team made a study of eighteen approved schools. They found that
absconding related to a number of factors relating to satisfaction or
lack of it within the residential establishment. They stated that a

good pastoral care system, particularly a climate in which boys felt able to discuss their personal problems with staff, moderated absconding. They went on to say:

There is overriding evidence that the environment and climate of the residential setting influences absconding behaviour. The regimes with high absconding seem to take in very delinquent boys, exercise low levels of institutional and expressive control and achieve poor levels of pastoral care and committment. On the other hand, regimes with low absconding rates have higher levels of control, happier boys, better pastoral care and seem to give less reinforcement to boys' delinquent aspirations so that if some boys do run away, they commit fewer offences. Such homes are also more willing than others to take back the returning child.

The main problem facing us when we started the 'hard-core' experiment was to divide absconding into two categories and to try and help both: casual and persistent. There was reason to hope that the manipulation of environmental variables may reduce casual or occasional absconding, but it was likely that the reduction of persistent absconding would probably require other measures. It was obvious that, in the early days, we would have to devise various tables and records to see if persistent absconding was linked to other factors. The first task, therefore, was to look closely at absconding figures for Ardale for a period of twelve months prior to the commencement of the 'hard-core' experiment and to later compare these with the experimental group. This took quite some time to collect and correlate: rather than give long lists of tables, some salient points are shown.

Facts re. absconding prior to the 'hard-core' experiment

1 The period taken was from 1 September 1973 - 31st August 1974.
2 42 per cent of the total school population absconded at least once.
3 10 per cent of the population were persistent absconders—they absconded five or more times in the year.
4 *Length of absconding*
Shown as percentages. Some boys appear more than once in the figures: (all percentages rounded to nearest whole number).

Absent less than two days	56
Absent for at least a week	12
Absent for two weeks plus	6

Absent for three weeks plus	8
Absent for at least a month	6
Absent for at least two months	4
Absent for at least three months	4
Absent for six months or more	3
Never located nor returned	2

5 7 per cent of the absconders returned to Ardale of their own accord.

6 The termination of the absconding, does not automatically indicate that the boy was returned to Ardale. There were approximately 25 per cent of the cases where the social worker decided that the boy would be better helped by remaining at home. In a number of cases, where the boys had obtained steady employment, we agreed, but there were cases where we felt the boy should have been returned. In fact, all the boys should have come back for a period before being allowed to leave as we felt that otherwise it merely reinforced the view that they could always get their own way if they tried hard enough.

In some cases the boys were apprehended as absconders for committing further offences. In quite a few of the cases boys returning from absconding admitted (or boasted) that they had carried out some form of crime without being discovered. The incidence of further criminality while an absconder at Ardale is shown in Table 9.1.

Table 9.1

Further criminality as an absconder

	%
Apprehended by police for committing an offence while an absconder.	33
Charged for the offence	16
Had other offences taken into consideration	4
Sent to Borstal for offences committed while an absconder.	11

If nothing else, the statistics in Table 9.1 show that the police are willing, in over half the cases, to drop charges if an absconder is returned to his CH(E).

7 Reasons given by the Ardale boys for absconding are shown in Table 9.2. In some cases more than one reason was given, but the main one only is shown. The reasons given by the boys only give a broad indication for absconding as almost every boy felt he had to justify himself—in many cases (e.g. being bullied) facts did not agree with a boys reason.

Table 9.2
Reasons given for absconding

	%
Bored, nothing to do, etc.	24
Being bullied or pressurised.	15
Worried about home or family situation	13
Worried about girl friend.	9
No intention of staying—usually new boys	11
For a lark or a bit of a giggle.	14
To deliberately commit offences	5
No specific reasons given nor elucidated.	9

(All percentages rounded to nearest whole number.)

Absconding statistics with the 'hard-core' group

Basic facts

This covered a period from August 1974 to August 1976 and initially took in fifty boys. Four of them left during or at the end of their initial two month trial period. For mathematical ease, Table 9.3 shows twenty-three coming into the scheme in 1974-75 and twenty-three in 1975-76. It is obvious that, in reality, there was a considerable overlap. In all cases, percentages have been rounded to the nearest whole number. For the sake of convenience, the two groups are referred to as year one and year two.

Table 9.3
Facts known prior to admission

	Year 1	Year 2
	%	%
Known history of school truanting.	48	44
Absconded from previous residential establishment.	12	15
Absconded from RAC.	11	13
Regarded as persistent absconder	22	27

Before the 'hard-core' group arrived it was, therefore gradually made known that half of them had been fairly regular school truants and a quarter of them were designated persistent absconders. The 13.3 per cent who had absconded from previous residential establishments were subjects of particular concern and it seemed that, in the early days of the experiment, Ardale had little more to offer that what they had previously absconded from. It seems clear that, to some extent, absconding is a learned habit.

Helping non-persistent 'hard-core' absconders

Following previous statistics and trends, it was assumed that we could expect about 40-45 per cent of the boys to abscond at least once during their stay at Ardale. Out of this, at least half would abscond within the first month. Statistics proved this assumption right in the first year when 47 per cent absconded, but there was some improvement in the second year when the figure was reduced to 34 per cent.

Table 9.4

Persistent absconders at Ardale 1974-76

	Year 1	Year 2
	%	%
The 'hard-core' group	18	7
The non 'hard-core' group	16	14

Once again, perhaps not very startling improvements, but with boys deemed to failure before they even arrived and many shown as persistent absconders by earlier reports, it was felt that our methods had done something to help break the pattern.

Offences as absconders committed by the 'hard-core' group

Although we managed to cut down the number of actual abscondings, both casual and persistent, the experiment had little or no effect on the numbers or types of offences committed by boys who did abscond. Four of the boys were sent to Borstal for offences committed as absconders from Ardale; six went to detention centres, although all six of them were returned to Ardale after completing their sentences.

Length of time as an absconder indicated, in most cases, the committing of offences. Apart from three boys, none of the 'hard-core' group who were missing for less than forty-eight hours, committed offences—or at least they were never caught or charged with committing offences which may be quite a different matter. Some of them did boast that they had done a job but there was no way of proving whether this was merely boasting or actual fact.

Taking the 'hard-core' group of absconders who were missing from between a week and six months, the bare facts look—and in fact were—very dismal (see Table 9.5).

Table 9.5
'Hard-core' group absconding offences

	%
Charged with one offence.	36
Charged with more than one offence.	21
Charged with three or more offences.	9

	As percentages of above
Offences relating to autocrime.	60
Offences of theft	22
Offences of personal violence	14
Other offences	4

Summary on 'hard-core' group absconding and offences

With the more personal regime offered to the 'hard-core' group it would appear that it is possible to decrease actual absconding. The fact that the boys knew that they would be received back, even if they had been sent to a detention centre for offences committed while absconding, probably did much to help the boys face up to the problems. The fact that absconding was not made a big emotive issue, but that boys who took time off unofficially would lose an equivalent amount of their own free time, also helped the boys in looking closely at their reasons for absconding.

Some boys, by the time they came to Ardale, were so set into a persistent absconding pattern that there was little or nothing we could do. However, in many cases, we were able to make inroads through discussion and personal help, into breaking absconding patterns. Nothing is mentioned about class differences as nothing significant came out of the research.

The general improvement of the 'hard-core' group in almost everything but the numbers and types of offences committed as absconders could perhaps indicate that absconding and criminality is not linked as many people think. Much more research is needed into the correlation between absconding and criminality.

'Internal' offences committed by the 'hard-core' group

It would be foolish to suppose that boys with such a past history of crime and violence would cease all criminal and violent activities merely because of the regime at Ardale.

Somebody once coined the phrase that there is honour amongst thieves, but this is completely untrue. Most of the young delinquents admitted to CH(E)s will steal from each other, will take every advantage of individual weaknesses, and will have no hesitation on grassing (informing) on their peers if it is to their personal advantage.

When the experiment began, it was expected that there would—initially at least—be an increase in internal theft and violence. Later in this book mention is made of the various problems staff had in coping with the experiment, but one of the main problems was the increase in petty crime and personal violence between boy and boy and, initially, between boy and staff. The main tool was, yet again, open and personal discussions about such activities. Group work played a vital role in getting boys to talk about each other's problems and gradually, as the experiment progressed, there was a definite diminuation in petty internal crimes. However, an occasional bout of very serious violence or vandalism did occur. One of the worst culminated in a boy being stabbed with a screwdriver which concluded with hospitalisation for one and Borstal for the other.

One of the few minor differences of opinion I had with some of the staff at Ardale was over allowing boys to put individual locks on their bedside lockers. The staff maintained that it gave the boys some sense of privacy and security, but I felt that it was encouraging a lack of trust between boys, and looked unsightly. The assortment of locks and padlocks around the bedrooms had to be seen to be believed. It was decided, however, with the experimental house to encourage honesty rather than security and all locks were removed. This was not met very well by the staff and the few remaining boys in Shackleton, but this was felt to be an opportunity to find out once and for all if it was possible with the really criminal type of boy to encourage them not to steal from each other. There may have been some occasions when a theft was carried out I did not hear about, or was sorted out by the boys themselves. However, we kept a detailed list of the numbers of offences of theft by boys from other boys' bedrooms and lockers (see Table 9.6).

Table 9.6

Number of thefts ('hard-core' group only)

	Number of thefts
October 1974	17
January 1975	19
May 1975	11
October 1975	7
January 1976	3
May 1976	0

Possibly it was indicated to the boys that they could take their chances of stealing outside the house, but it must never happen within. In effect, we created a tradition of honesty amongst the 'hard-core' group.

Many boys do silly things in moments of great stress. Anger is an emotion that can be so spontaneous it is unpredictable. Frustration and a build up of pressure can be noted and controlled, but sheer raw anger must be dealt with as it arises. The actual cause may be quite trivial, but the consequences can be completely out of proportion. One of the 'hard-core' boys had been refused a day pass one Saturday following a week of stupid behaviour in the classroom. He came to see me to have the decision reversed, but I turned down his request and told him that his behaviour had not merited any special privileges. He walked out of my office and pulled down a complete wall that had been built that week by the building department. When I saw him later, he was completely contrite and apologetic. He spent most of Sunday labouring to my building instructor who was on weekend duty rebuilding the wall he had damaged.

One of the criteria for success was that crime within Ardale should diminish. This was not only evident from statistics as recorded, but from general observation. Many social workers and parents of the 'hard-core' group stated that they had noted a general improvement in behaviour. By using every available means, the staff dealing primarily with the 'hard-core' group, did tend to lower the incidence of internal petty crime, vandalism and violence.

10   Staff, social workers and parents

Although I link social workers, Ardale staff, and the boys' parents together, the problems, views and general attitudes were quite dissimilar in many respects. The problems experienced by social workers and parents were predominantly ones of expectation rather than one of care and control as was the case with the staff. Working and living with delinquent boys in a residential setting for twenty-four hours a day is a difficult, demanding, and frequently unrewarding task: working with the 'hard-core' category in similar circumstances was, sometimes, almost unbearable.

Social workers

Although CH(E) workers are sometimes referred to as residential social workers, the majority prefer to call themselves merely residential workers. For the purpose of this chapter, the term social worker is used specifically to refer to field social workers as distinct from residential workers.

The difference in training opportunities, salaries, promotion prospects, and general esteem between social workers and residential workers is quite well known. What is not so often publicised is the even greater gap between different categories of residential workers. In all respects, those that work in CH(E)s are in division one. In some cases, e.g. house wardens, CH(E) residential staff are actually much better off in most respects than many of their colleagues in the field. All of Ardale's untrained staff get opportunities to go on full training courses: quite a number of the residential staff earn in excess of £5,000 per annum in addition to subsidised housing. This does not infer that the latter is a perk as most of the staff have no choice but to live on the premises, but it has to be taken into account when considering ways of life and standards of living.

Much has been done over the past few years to help both social workers and residential workers to understand the problems of the other. The two specific aspects which were of concern during the 'hard-core' experiment, were those of co-operation and attitudes of the boys. The former mainly concerned contact with the school on such matters as case reviews, home leave, etc. The social worker had a very real role to play in relation to Ardale in general and the specific child in particular. This role can best be described as an integrative and supportive one.

The attitude of the boys' to their social workers has always been an important one and one which residential workers have not always done their best to foster. It has sometimes been forgotten that, in many cases, the social worker has known the boy for much longer and is a very real link in the contact between home, normality, and Ardale. Many of the boys feel guilty about the relationships they have with their parents: they blame themselves for such things as parents separating. The social worker visits the home, knows the parents and is perhaps the only person who has a foot in both camps—home and Ardale. The frequently heard claim that it is the social worker that had a boy sent to a CH(E) can never be taken at its face value. Observation has shown over a period of years, that there is very often a love/hate relationship between a boy in Ardale and his social worker. This does not refer to the sexual aspect many boys like to quote when discussing some of the more attractive female social workers. This is, almost always, as much wishful thinking on the boy's part as is his feeling towards the attractive female residential worker. No, what is meant is that a boy may lay some of the blame on his social worker for the actual application for a care order, but he also realises that this person usually really cares what happens to him. Of course there are poor social workers exactly as there are their equivalents in the residential service. Social work is struggling to be regarded as a worthwhile profession. At the moment it is fighting a hard battle. Most of the work done by social workers is ignored, but let a baby be battered or an old lady burn herself to death and then see what the average member of the public thinks of social workers. It is for this reason so few residential workers really like to be called residential social workers.

There has always been a fairly high level of committment between the school and the social worker when a boy has been admitted to Ardale. With the 'hard-core' group this was of an even higher standard. It was known that unless it was an obvious fact, clearly seen by the boy, that the social worker and Ardale's staff were on a firm professional basis, any rift could and would be used to the boy's advantage. We decided to encourage the 'hard-core' group to personally persuade their social workers to visit more frequently and to take part in group activities. Not a lot of the social workers did actually join in group work but we maintained that it was much better for the boys to suggest it initially than the staff. The boys knew this and were always told to let their social workers know that they could check it out with us first. Now we have commenced a new admissions policy, we make it clear from the start that the role of the social worker has to be far greater, and insist they visit before a boy is admitted.

One of the problems with social workers is that there appears to be a greater turnover than with residential workers. This may be because there are more opportunities for promotion. It does, however, cause problems. A boy who has a number of social workers in a short space of time tends to have a completely different attitude to a boy who has had one social worker for many years. It is difficult to explain that social workers really care when they move on to other posts.

One of the biggest difficulties experienced with social workers of the 'hard-core' group was of my own making. I had not really sold the idea beforehand of what we hoped to achieve with the boys. To the majority of them it merely appeared that Ardale was a CH(E) which would take a lad other CH(E)s had refused. There was very little indication that anything positive was going to be attempted. Most social workers were so relieved to get the boy fixed up some-where, even though it may be only for two months, that they did not want to complicate matters by asking such questions as 'What is he going to do?' or 'Can Ardale help him with his problems?' I did not sell what I hoped to do, even though I knew that nothing succeeds like success and that word of mouth comments between social workers can greatly influence which particular CH(E) is thought good and which bad. Quite a number of social workers became aware of what we were trying to do, but they should have known because they had been told in advance. If nothing else, this is a lesson we learned the hard way.

Parents

Social workers and residential workers have in general a very jaundiced view on the parents of delinquent children. We too frequently create stereotypes and regard the parents as statistics that get in the way of letting us professionals get on with the job of caring for children. As a body, we really are an egocentric group of people. We tend to look at the parent of a delinquent child in care as a person who has absolutely no rights and must come to us cap in hand for what scraps of information we throw out. A little bit of experience and perhaps a little bit of training, and we create this god like complex that we know better than the parents when it comes to all matters of child care.

Every parent of every child in care has at least one specific pro-blem or the child would not be in care: it may be a physical one, an emotional one, a psychiatric one, or one caused by any number of other factors. The problems of the parent of a delinquent child are usually much more complex. Frequently they feel guilty themselves for the activities which brought their child to court. Sometimes they are, but the whole system encourages them to continue to feel guilty. In casual conversations over many years, the subject of what causes delinquency has been broached with me many times. Usually, I throw the question back. In at least seven cases out of ten, the standard answer throws the complete blame on the parents.

Very few parents actually visit CH(E)s. This statement is absolutely true, but how many people who make it attempt to analyse why? To start with, how many parents are actively encouraged by social workers and CH(E) staff to visit and take part in activities? I use the word actively with great meaning. We all send out circulars about Open Days and Christmas festivities. Many of us forget that to some of our parents letters coming into the home are infrequent events and can be quite threatening. To actively encourage a parent to visit means that a member of Ardale's staff visits the home and discusses what is happening to their son: this may then be followed up by a promise to collect them from home or from the station when we would like them to visit.

The parents of many delinquent children and almost all first generation West Indian parents have a certain degree of respect and/or fear for teachers. As most CH(E) staff are seen as teachers by the parents it is our job to let the parents know that we are also human and not some robots computed to improving their children's behaviour. When we talk to parents, it is fatal to have them in an office. We want to talk to parents not at them. The best place to meet them is in their own homes: when this is not possible, some neutral ground is advisable. I usually invite the parents to have a walk around the grounds with me.

Many of us are so jargon orientated, that we actually begin to believe that by calling a spade an implement for the purpose of moving earth or similar material, we are being helpful. Our job is to convince the parents that we really are trying to help their sons, not to show them what clever and educated people we are by the use of such phrases as therapeutic concepts.

Delinquency and crime runs in the family. That is another well worn phrase. Of course it does in some cases, but not as a genetic disease. Some families have discovered that crime really does pay. It may not pay very much but it is certainly better than working for a living. These parents, however, are definitely in the minority. Well over two-thirds of the parents of delinquent children have never been caught committing anything much more serious than parking on a yellow line or driving up a one way street. They are at a loss to understand why their son has so shamed them by taking up crime. They blame the schools, the environment, the permissive society, even the police; but deep in their own hearts they are blaming themselves.

With the 'hard-core' group, we went out of our way to have a far greater contact with the parents than in the past. Those that would not, or could not visit Ardale were visited in their own homes. I personally visited about a third of them and would have liked the time to visit them all. Sometimes I went with the social worker, but the most profitable visits I had was when I took the boy home and asked him if I could come in and 'have a chat with mum'. The lad himself had usually done the spade work anyway by talking about the school and the staff during other periods at home.

When we are denigrating parents we usually forget that they are still the focal point of a boy's life and, in most cases, the people they will be returning to when they leave Ardale. When we encourage boys in such social graces as not eating from a knife or drinking tea out of a saucer we would be foolish to think they will stop doing it at home if dad eats his peas from his knife and mum slops tea out of a saucer. What we hope is that when they are married and have families themselves, they will remember that although dad eats peas from his knife it is not the accepted fashion, even though most of his family may think it is. This is one of those long term seeds which may or may not bear fruit and which we shall never know any way in almost every case.

It is true that many parents have a low tolerance level with the criminal and behavioural activities of their sons when they are at home. Absence may make the heart grow fonder, but some parents need long absences from their delinquent and criminal offspring. With all the 'hard-core' group, it was made absolutely clear that if they caused problems at home when on leave and their parents requested they went home less frequently, these wishes would be carried out. Parents were encouraged to let us know about the behaviour of their sons and, according to the parents, the 'hard-core' group were at least as well behaved at home as the other boys at Ardale and, in many cases, much better. This may have been because they had more to lose, but the closer co-operation between Ardale staff and the parents of the 'hard-core' group certainly had positive results.

If there is tripartite co-operation between school, parent and social worker it is often possible to help a boy despite himself. If the parents believe in what the school is doing and actively encourage a boy to do his best, many of the problems are considerably minimised. I will conclude this section with a comment made to me by the father of one of my 'hard-core' boys: 'I thought nobody could ever help him, but somehow you have got through to him. I wish you'd tell me how'.

Ardale staff

> The staff of a community home need to create and maintain an environment where children, including those who are very disturbed and difficult, can feel welcome, comfortable and safe. Such an environment can encourage the growth of personal relationships between children and adults, enabling the staff to provide support for the children while helping them to cope with their individual problems and to face the implications of disturbing behaviour. (HMS), 1970)

Like any theory the above sentiment is easy to write but much more difficult to put into practice. There are a fantastic number of variables which influence day to day relationships between boys and staff at Ardale or any other CH(E). I have already explained how I carefully chose the right staff to operate the experimental scheme and to work with the 'hard-core' boys in Shackleton. This in itself was not too difficult a task: the problem came with some of the other staff. No member of staff would be able to isolate him or herself from the influences and possible conflicts of the 'hard-core' boys.

It is of paramount importance when planning any scheme such as this to have sufficient staff. One of the most positive results arising from the experiment has been a full survey and a considerable increase in Ardale staffing. At the time of operating the experimental scheme, Ardale was certainly considerably under staffed.

It is imperative that the roles of all staff should be clearly defined. Even this is difficult, as no member of staff in a CH(E) plays one specific role. Some roles appear distinctive, but in fact are far more complex. A teacher teaches, but what when he stops to drink a cup of tea and chat to a lad, or when he has to organise evening activities, or when he takes a couple of boys to his home at the weekend to help him in the garden?

Only if staff fully understand their basic roles can they be fully integrated into a CH(E). The lack of knowledge of a member of staff's role is frequently the main reason for a breakdown in communication. It is an easy task to prepare a job description, but this only gives the bare bones of the mammoth task facing a new member of staff. Autonomy and delegation have to be clearly understood. Staff have to know just how much responsibility they have before referring to the next person up the ladder. Staff need to have the insight and skill to know what specialist advice and help is required and available, especially when they are working alongside visiting consultant specialists.

Perhaps the most important element of all is job satisfaction. Successful staff enjoy their work. Of course, there are frustrating times, but basic happiness in the class room or the house unit is of paramount importance. No matter how experienced a member of staff is, when he first arrives at a CH(E) he is seen by the boys as a new boy. It quickly becomes obvious to the children that some new staff are only new to Ardale and that they know the ropes. Completely inexperienced staff, whether they be residential workers or teachers, however, almost always have a very difficult first term or two. The good ones soon establish themselves as personalities and any member of staff who is still going through a baptism of fire six months after his appointment is highly unlikely to ever make the grade in a CH(E). It is very difficult to talk about job satisfaction with a member of staff who has not found his level.

I frequently tell my new staff when they are going through a particularly difficult patch that they cannot automatically copy a more experienced person's approach and expect it to work for them: they must develop their own approach and personality, although they should be able to adapt various methods used by other staff to their own advantage. Quite a number of young staff take some time to accept this. 'Why is it', they say, 'that when Mr So-and-so tells the boys to sit down and listen to him they do, but when I tell them, they just ignore me?' We have all gone through this stage at some time or another. Professional qualifications may help a person to obtain an appointment to a CH(E) but nothing is as important as experience. The only snag is that you can only get experience by getting experience!! Once a member of staff can say to himself: 'I remember a similar experience five years ago', or 'that 'con' was tried on me many years ago', then he has the necessary experience to at least survive. Unless a member of staff can feel he is doing a worthwhile job and that it is not a constant losing battle, he will achieve no job satisfaction.

The particular problems of female staff in Ardale

It was almost a tradition in boys' approved schools that the dominion of care and control was almost exclusively a masculine one. Female teachers were almost unique and housemothers were glorified domestics. This attitude was, if not liked, accepted by most female staff

116

and was self perpetuating. The chauvinistic autocracy of the males in approved schools was transmitted to the boys. Very few boys would regard a housemother as a person who did much more than dish out food, wash socks and change laundry. This was a situation I inherited when taking over Ardale in 1973. Female staff considerably under functioned, through no fault of their own, in the approved school days.

A housemother, or female residential worker, call her what you will, has a specific role to play in her house. She must be capable— and allowed—to assist in organisation, planning, administration and group activities. It is essential that she should be able to freely discuss each boy with other members of staff, social workers and parents. In most cases she will wish to detach herself from an authoritarian role and become more of a counsellor, but this is not always so. There are very few roles which, in the past, have been accepted as masculine which an experienced and competent female cannot carry out just as well. The old ideas about a woman not being capable of seeing the boys to bed or getting them up in the morning is completely outmoded.

A good female residential worker should be able to help the boys with the problems they have with relationships. She must also learn that there will be some boys who, for various reasons, wish to have nothing to do with a female member of staff or wish to confide in other members of staff both male and female. She should, however, particularly in the group situation, be on the lookout for boys who seem disturbed or distressed and in need of individual attention which can best be provided by the feminine approach.

It is important that female staff should be very involved in the admission process, and it has already been shown how the housemother approached this with the 'hard-core' group in Shackleton House. Boys are extremely vulnerable when they first arrive and at this stage a relationship can be formed which is extremely valuable, therapeutic and lasting. Many of the boys have poor opinions of themselves and it is a very important part of the female role to treat them as individuals and show them that she is there to help them.

Staff reactions to the 'hard-core' group

Chapter 7 has already dealt in some detail with the behavioural evaluation of the staff directly concerned with the 'hard-core' experiment. What it does not show is the general feeling of the total professional staff. It was expected that the sudden input of very difficult, acting-out, and aggressive boys would cause change and change is both threatening and vulnerable to traditional patterns of child care. Without their actually knowing it, I continually monitored staff responses to the system. This was done by making notes after every discussion with staff about the system, no matter how trivial. We have seen that those staff directly concerned with the experiment altered their views over a two year period and generally felt that it was a success. What about the other staff? I formed a list of questions which I managed to slip into the conversation at some time or another with all teaching and residential staff not directly concerned with the 'hard-core group.

1 Within two months of admitting the first 'hard-core' boy, I posed the question: 'What do you think of the idea?' The results came out as follows:

	Teaching Staff	Residential Staff
	%	%
It is a good idea	12	30
It might work	24	20
It is a bad idea	48	40
No feelings expressed	16	10

2 I asked the same question to basically the same group of staff after approximately eighteen months: 'Do you think the idea has worked?'

	Teaching Staff	Residential Staff
	%	%
Yes it has worked	24	25
It has worked for some boys only	24	25
It has not worked	36	40
No feelings expressed	16	10

Obviously I was somewhat disappointed in the majority of replies to my first questionning and even more disappointed to the later response. In both cases I tried to find out why so many staff expected failure and, later, felt that the system had failed. The responses of teachers and other staff would, I felt be different, but I was seeking some common denominator. I attempted to elucidate the particular problems both categories of staff felt was causing such a low success predictability rate. Over a period of time, it was possible to draw up what I called the problem priorities (see Table 10.1).

Table 10.1

Staff not directly responsible for the experimental scheme: initially asked to estimate problems in October 1974, and later in April 1976. Priorities in order of five with one being the highest as seen by each group

Priorities	Teachers		Male Housestaff		Female Housestaff	
	Oct. 1974	Apr. 1976	Oct. 1974	Apr. 1976	Oct. 1974	Apr. 1976
Violence amongst peers		3		1	2	2
Violence to staff	3		5	2	1	3
Bullying	2	1	4			1
Classroom violence	1				3	
Vandalism		4			4	
Racial problems	5		1		5	
Insolence to staff		2	3			4
Absconding	4		2		4	5
Theft in school		5	3		5	

Priority ratings

It must be emphasised again that Table 10.1 only deals with those members of staff not directly concerned with the experimental scheme in Shackleton. There was one other category mentioned by two members of staff: an increase of theft in the locality. In both cases, this has been linked with an increase of theft in the school. One or two points are perhaps worth specific mention:

1 Only one category—bullying—actually receives top priority twice. Both the teachers and the female staff rated this the highest problem after the scheme had been in operation for eighteen months.
2 Violence to peers and to staff takes a high priority in all groups. Only the teachers felt that violence to staff was not as high as they had expected. Perhaps the main reason it is rated so highly with the male staff is that a housemaster had been hit by a boy shortly before I asked my question. Although the female staff still rate this, there was no actual incident of any physical violence to any female member of the housestaff, although one of my female Community Service Volunteers had been attempted to be sexually molested.
3 All groups predicted racial problems as being a priority concern at the first time of asking, but none regarded it as materialising. This is perhaps a significant point which seems to

bear out the theory that most of the racial violence in CH(E)s is caused by having minority groups. With our ratio of almost one for one, there was never any specific racial problem. A number of coloured boys were troublesome problems, but this was in no way related to the colour of their skin.

4 All categories thought that the 'hard-core' group were much more insolent than they had originally predicted.

5 Absconding estimates are as to be expected, although male housestaff show an actual decline in the pattern.

Conclusions on staff attitudes

Weighing up what we know now, I doubt very much if I would have involved many more of my staff, as it was then, in the scheme. There were perhaps one or two staff who could have been more involved, but in the main, I feel that I chose the right staff for the experiment. Perhaps it is best to conclude this section with a few comments made and recorded towards the end of the scheme from members of staff not directly involved. For the sake of confidentiality, I give their title rather than their name:

> I'm glad it is over. It was never fair on us staff to have so many problem boys at the same time. We've had a hard time here. (*Instructor*)

> We have had too many coloured kids in the school. They think they're running the place. (*Teacher*)

> Perhaps somebody can do something now to cut down all the bullying. (*Housemaster*)

> It's been like sitting on a volcano. (*Housemaster*)

> You know when ..... attacked that CSV girl, it could have happened to any of us. (*Housemother*)

> Some of the lads were much better than we expected. I don't know why we are stopping taking them. If we do take any more really difficult boys, I would like to be more involved. (*Housemother*)

11   Follow-up research

There is a so-called 'statistic' that 70 per cent of children passing through CH(E)s are failures. Although the Ardale experiment was initially formulated to see if it was possible to really help the 'hard-core' delinquent within a CH(E), sufficient time has now elapsed to evaluate the scheme at a much wider level. Detailed statistics of school leavers were kept and, in early 1979, it became possible to correlate these.

The first problem to face was the knowledge that quite a number of disturbed adolescents grow up to attain a quite well adjusted adult life. Clarizo and McCoy state:

> In our present state of knowledge, we can conclude that there is at best only mild or moderate evidence to support the notion that disturbed children turn into seriously disturbed adults. The conception of emotional disturbance in children as a progressively deteriorating condition is thus called into question. (Clarizo and McCoy, 1970)

If emotional disturbance in adolescence is the only criteria to judge success or failure it is often extremely difficult, or even impossible to evaluate any specific method of help or treatment. However, I have always believed in what I refer to as the CH(E) placebo effect. In simple terms, this means that a CH(E) can be regarded as a pill made out of sugar—it may have no obvious curative effect on a child, but because he or she thinks that it has, the positive effect is the same. This is true of all children entering residential establishments where there is a positive atmosphere. The danger in evaluating specifically the 'hard-core' group, was to be continually aware of the placebo effect and not let it get in the way of rational analysis.

Before starting to correlate all the information collected between 1974-79, a list was drawn up to enable us to evaluate success or failure based on the experimental scheme. Obviously it was necessary to carry out a similar check on a sample of boys admitted at roughly the same time as the bulk of the experimental group. Well knowing the very wise saying that there are 'lies, damned lies, and statistics', it was absolutely essential to deal with every one of the fifty boys who were deemed 'hard-core' or a true picture would not be obtained. It would have been very easy to take a random (or deliberately non-random) sample from the group of fifty and prove anything.

Follow-up with the non 'hard-core' group was initially deemed much less of a problem as it did not really matter which boys were used provided they were admitted at roughly the same time as the main experimental group. In practice, this sometimes proved even more difficult. If nothing else, I learned that the commitment of individual social workers to the boys in the experimental group had, in the main, been far more reaching than the general remainder. It became quite clear that if the system were to be re-introduced, individual social workers must become more involved from the very beginning. As described later, the results of the experiment partly contributed to a complete reappraisal of Ardale, and a much more intensive liaison with social workers before a boy is even admitted, has been built into our new programme.

In my original hypotheses, it was stated that the Ardale 'hard-core' experiment should hopefully show a marked pattern of improvement, in relation to previous criminal history, of the boys involved in the experiment after they had left Ardale, provided they left in normal circumstances. Linked with this hypothesis were the criteria of success after leaving Ardale. Obviously, the general public and even many researchers into CH(E)s regard success and failure of the CH(E) system to revolve entirely around reconviction rates. To a certain extent this is a natural and quite correct action to take. It would be a very foolish CH(E) principal who talked about the success of his boys when most of them were inside Borstal or prison. Obviously further criminality must be taken into very serious consideration when evaluating the results of this type of experiment. As stated earlier the following was a basic guideline:

> To be judged a success as far as criminality was concerned, a boy from the experimental group must not receive from any court, for at least one year after leaving Ardale, any custodial sentence. Nor, on the same basis, could he appear in court more than once (except for remands or adjournments) on *any* charge whether the sentence be custodial or otherwise.

This very rigid outline—used for evaluating results with the sample non 'hard-core' group too—was sufficiently positive to give some definite results as far as criminality itself went. Many people reading this may say that one year was not sufficient, but some guideline had to be made. Would it really be fair to the group, using the criteria of a maximum of one court appearance, to suggest that in, say five years, a young man had received two parking tickets and was therefore a failure of the Ardale experiment?

Obviously there are many other factors used to define the success or failure of the experiment, but it is probably best if I initially use the criteria most expected in analysing such a scheme—further or continuing criminality. In many cases, I am indebted to those social workers who kept me informed as to the progress of the boys for quite lengthy periods after they had left Ardale. In one or two cases the social worker had ceased contact with the case but was only too willing to check with his successor and let me know the results. Naturally, those boys sent to a detention centre were made known by the fact that in all such cases, the detention centres themselves contact the original CH(E) for information.

Statistics relating to continuing criminality

Methodology

The 'hard-core' group of fifty boys. Of the original fifty boys, six (12 per cent) left during the course of the experiment. These were deemed failures and did not concern much further research. Four of them went to Borstal directly from Ardale and two of them went permanently missing and never returned. The six failures of the system were checked to see if they had anything in common. Counting the first boy into the experiment as number one and the last boy as number fifty, the internal failures were numbered eight, fourteen, twenty-three, thirty-four, thirty-six and forty-four. Obviously, apart from the two in the thirties, it could not be said that any particular failure influenced the others. All six of the boys were between the ages of fifteen and sixteen and a half, but as this is the average age period for boys in a senior CH(E), it was felt that this had little or no relevance. Only two of the six failures were non-white boys. Five of the six came from broken homes, and all of them had absconded at least twice while at Ardale. Apart, then, from the latter two facts, there was no significant correlation between the six boys who failed to complete the experiment.

The sample group of twenty-five boys. Eventually, in the interest of pure random sampling techniques, I decided to use my original group C. These were twenty-five boys who had been admitted during the course of the experiment and were, by my definition, normal CH(E) boys. Normal means that they did not show the overt signs and attitudes which placed a boy in the 'hard-core' category. The first pertinent fact observed was that three of the boys—i.e. 12 per cent—had not completed the period of training at Ardale. All three had been sent for a period of further custodial training; two to Borstal and one to DC who was not re-admitted because of the problems he was causing to his peers. So, there was exactly the same percentage of normal boys as 'hard-core boys who failed to complete their training at Ardale. This, in itself was very significant. Was it because the Ardale experiment was working, or was it because the original assessment for both categories of boy had been at fault?

Obtaining information

This was the most difficult and time consuming part of the entire experiment. As previously mentioned, there was a great deal of co-operation from many social workers but, in some cases, the results were completely negative. It was felt desirable not to produce questionnaires but to seek information on a more personal basis. DC and Borstal requests for information gave a clear indication of those boys who had received further and more intense custodial sentences.

Many of the boys from CH(E)s, contrary to popular myth, love to keep in touch with the establishment. It is very rare for a week-end to go by without at least one 'old boy' visiting. It was thus possible to get reasonably accurate information about many of the boys from our visitors. Often they would not be too honest about their own activities, but they were only too eager to tell me that 'so and so is in court again next week for nicking cars'. In addition, with most of the boys coming from the London boroughs, it was not difficult to ask a boy how a boy who had left was getting on. With the verbal information given, it was usually possible to check later through the various social service agencies.

Much of the information which was eventually accumulated depended upon telephone calls to social workers. All in all, there was about a 95 per cent response which was sufficient to form some basis for working out statistics, (see Table 11.1).

The results are extremely significant and seem completely contrary to everything we all expected. Even working on the assumption that the unknowns in the 'hard-core' group were failures and the unknowns in the normal group were successes, the figures, based on further court appearances only, show a success rate of 38.5 per cent for the 'hard-core' group as against 48.5 per cent for the normal group. If we ignore the two unknowns in the 'hard-core' group the percentage could be shown as 43.2 per cent. Let us take a look at what some of the above statistics appear to indicate. It must be remembered that the definition of a failure of the system is making more than one court appearance where the sentence is non-custodial. Significantly, it must also be remembered at all times that these are court appearances only. There is no way of recording successful crime where the culprit avoided detection and arrest.

Table 11.1

Further criminality in first twelve months

	'Hard-core' Group (44)		Normal Group (22)	
	No.	%	No.	%
Boys receiving custodial sentence	8	18.3	3	13.6
Boys making two or more court appearances (excluding above)	17	38.5	9	49.9
No information available	2	4.7	3	12.7

However, no official statistics can accurately record undetected juvenile crime. The usual publicised failure rate of CH(E)s based on further apprehended criminality only is stated as being 70 per cent. With the 'hard-core' group, this was expected to be even possibly higher. Being ultra-pessimistic and assuming that all the unknown were failures, it would appear that either the national statistics are wrong or Ardale must be somewhere near the top of the league. With 38.5 per cent of the 'hard-core' group being successful and, at the most pessimistic, 32.8 per cent of the normal group, but more likely 45.5 per cent showing similar success, Ardale appears to be above the national failure rate for boys leaving CH(E)s.

Perhaps the most significant finding is that, pro rata, the 'hard-core' group did as well as the normal intake. Did this, then, indicate, that the methods used in the Ardale experiment had partly succeeded? Do not forget that it has been assumed that the two unknowns in the 'hard-core' group were failures. There is no evidence whatsoever to prove or disprove this, but it could quite easily be that the success rate of the 'hard-core' group, based on further court appearances alone was as high as 43 per cent. This is well above the usual quoted (and misquoted) statistics.

One of the continual arguments used in favour of what are called alternatives to residential training is that the high cost of CH(E)s does not justify the very low success rate. Those who work in CH(E)s have to live with this negative outlook although so far none of the so called alternatives have shown any better success and, in many cases, much less. Based exclusively on this very minor piece of research in one senior boys' CH(E), it is time that a complete re-appraisal was made of what a positive CH(E) has to offer those boys for whom no alternative resource is available. If nothing else, the findings indicate a continued need for CH(E) placement for a certain type and percentage of difficult delinquent child.

Table 11.2 is based on the court appearances of the twenty-five out of forty-four 'hard-core' group and the twelve out of twenty-two normal group. The only cases where more than one type of offence were committed were when motoring offences were combined with theft. A boy who stole a car was charged not only with theft, but various statutes such as driving uninsured. To avoid any percentile complications, merely the number of offences are stated, as six of the 'hard-core' group and two of the normal group made three court appearances, the final one culminating in a custodial sentence. In all, there were fifty-six court appearances with the 'hard-core' group and twenty-six with the normal group. In those cases where other offences have been taken into consideration, only the main offence the boy has been charged with is statistically recorded.

Table 11.2

The types of offences committed

Offences	'Hard-core'	Normal
Motoring offences only	9	4
Motoring offences and theft	6	4
All other forms of theft	21	11
All forms of assault (including mugging)	9	1
Drink offences	10	6
Attempted rape	1	0

As expected, various forms of theft, including car thefts, take up the main bulk of the court appearances (48 per cent and 68 per cent). Of the ten cases of assault, six were of a mugging nature. All six were committed by coloured boys, and of the other four, three were common assault, and one sexual assault, two of these (including the sexual assault) carried out by coloured boys. The attempted rape was also committed by a West Indian boy. Whether or not there is any significance in this, using such a small sample, I cannot say.

It is of considerable significance that 18 per cent of the 'hard-core' groups and 23 per cent of the normal group were taken to court for offences relating to alcoholism. What is perhaps even more significant is the fact that no boy from either group appeared in any court for any activity relating to drugs. There is little doubt that drink is causing a greater number of problems with delinquent boys than drugs. Obviously the latter is much more serious, but just how long can we continue to ignore the facts about teenage drinking?

Conclusions on further criminality

In the main, the sample or normal group keeps very much to what is expected by the national statistics. The fact that they are slightly better than expected could, with such a small sample mean exactly nothing. However, it is possible that the few per cent of successes above the national average is directly attributable to what we had to offer at Ardale.

The general results with the 'hard-core' group, on the other hand, are more than promising. They exceed what all concerned expected. If a 70 per cent failure rate is the norm with the average CH(E) boy, it would have been logical to expect 80-90 per cent failure on further criminality alone with a group of boys who were deemed failures before they entered Ardale. One significant factor, not shown by the tables is that, on the whole, the white boys involved in the experiment succeeded better than the coloured boys in regard to further court appearances. Approximately 65 per cent of the 'hard-core' group shown in tables one and two were coloured boys. This, however, could reflect the attitude of society much more clearly than merely stating that the black 'hard-core' boy was a failure. On the basis of further criminality, the experiment was quite successful.

Statistics relating to employment

Although an outline of further criminality has been given first, as this tends to be regarded by most people as the only criteria for defining success and failure, the most important factor in my estimation was the ability of the boys to obtain and keep regular employment. Even in this era of mass unemployment, most CH(E) boys are capable of finding some form of employment.

Only two boys from the 'hard-core' group and none from the sample group returned to normal state education during the course of their stay at Ardale. A check on the two boys concerned in 1979 showed both had left school and both were in regular employment. Therefore, for the following statistics, all reference is to the total group, apart from the six who fell out of the system by failing to complete it.

Once again, the method of obtaining information was gained by a similar means to that for gleaning other statistics. However, this time there were two advantages. In every case of a boy leaving for employment we knew the name of the firm he was going to work for. Similarly, all Ardale boys know that they can quote my name as a reference if they wish to change their employment. In most cases information was gleaned from boys or social workers but on about a dozen occasions we telephoned the firms direct for details. There were a few—a very small minority—who failed to gain a job during their period of employment leave and who had been taken off Ardale's books after a lengthy period for fiscal reasons. However, in all cases, it was possible to gain information from the respective social service departments.

Perhaps it is necessary to explain what is meant by employment leave. When it is decided, following a case review, that any Ardale boy is ready to leave he initially goes out to seek employment while still remaining on the register. As the place is kept open and the local authority fully charged for the place, there is some need to stipulate a time limit in most cases, varying from two to eight weeks, with the norm being about a month. Many boys obtain employment almost as soon as they go home, but it is a useful safeguard to see how they go on for a week or so before finally removing their names from the operative register. If a boy cannot or will not obtain employment he is usually returned to try again in a few weeks time. Only on very rare occasions does a social worker request that a boy remain at home, come off books and be unemployed. The lads know this and it therefore makes them even more anxious to obtain employment. There are, as statistics show, a few who use this system to their own nefarious advantage by obtaining a job just long enough to come off the register and then going on the dole. This, fortunately, is the exception rather than the rule. The original hypothesis regarding employment states: 'To obtain and keep employment for at least one year after leaving Ardale. This does not preclude a boy from changing employment, but not too frequently and for valid reasons only'. We later decided to try to find out just how many boys had taken up, kept or changed to a form of employment based on the various vocational subjects taught at Ardale. It was felt that this could give some guideline as to the need to continue or modify what Ardale had to offer. At that time, there was no motor mechanics nor painting and decorating department, both of which were created directly relative to the numbers of boys who had obtained employment in this sphere. We later disbanded plumbing and plastering as figures proved that hardly any boys were using what they had been taught at Ardale to seek employment in these spheres.

As a side issue, a look was taken at the percentages of boys who had used their academic qualifications of GCE or CSE to any real advantage in seeking employment where these were criteria for obtaining the job or necessary for the proper implementation of the work. The results were so negative and disappointing that it was felt the old image of Ardale being a grammar school type of CH(E) was a complete waste of time and needed altering quickly.

The sample groups

A *The 'hard-core' group.* Of the original fifty, six left while still at Ardale, eight received custodial sentences in their first year and could therefore not be regarded as being successful in obtaining and keeping employment, and two boys we have not been able to trace. Figures, therefore relating to employment are based on a total of thirty-four boys.

B *The sample group.* Of the original twenty-five boys, three left while still at Ardale, three received custodial sentences in their first year, and information is not known on three of them. Figures, therefore, relating to employment are based on a total of sixteen boys.

Table 11.3

Employment situation at end of year

| | 'Hard-core' | | Normal | |
	No.	%	No.	%
In full-time employment at end of first year	27	79.5	11	68.5
Unemployed at end of first year	7	20.5	5	31.5

Table 11.4

Number of jobs in first year

| | 'Hard-core' | | Normal | |
	No.	%	No.	%
One job only	8	23.5	3	18.75
Two jobs	11	32.5	4	24.5
Three jobs	5	15.00	3	18.75
More than three jobs	3	8.75	1	6.5
Unemployed	7	20.5	5	31.5

Table 11.5

Reasons for leaving first job

	'Hard-core' 19 boys	Normal 8 boys
Dismissed	2	0
Left of own accord (various reasons given)	12	6
To seek better job and obtained one	5	2

Table 11.6

Length of time after leaving Ardale before obtaining employment

	'Hard-core' 27 boys	Normal 11 boys
Less than a week	18	6
1 to 4 weeks	5	2
4 to 8 weeks	2	1
8 to 12 weeks	2	0
Over 12 weeks	0	2

Table 11.7

Types of employment first obtained

	'Hard-core' 27 boys	Normal 11 boys
Motor trade/garage work	9	4
Building trade	6	3
Factory work	5	1
Shop work or market trading	5	2
Other employment	2	1

An analysis of the employment statistics

Table 11.3. If one of the criteria for a successful CH(E) boy is to obtain employment, then all the Ardale boys were successful. Not having national statistics for school leavers from state comprehensive schools, it is still possible to assume that the Ardale boys are at least as good as the national average for school leavers in obtaining employment. Obviously only a small sample is shown in the various tables, but a quick check through Ardale's records shows that for the past twelve months (July 1978 to July 1979), over 65 per cent of all the boys leaving Ardale obtained employment within four weeks of leaving. If nothing else, this perhaps speaks well for the system of employment leave in which boys know they will be returned to Ardale unless they find work. My personal view is that work is available for school leavers but so many are pre-conditioned into thinking that they will not get a job and so few pressures are put on them, that they do not try hard enough. If over six out of every ten boys who leave a CH(E) can obtain a job, do not tell me that a similar ratio cannot be obtained by boys leaving a comprehensive school.

The most heart warming fact from Table 11.3 is that of the group which was deemed to failure from the start, their end results *viz a viz*

130

employment were even better than the normally assessed groups. Once again, it must be stressed that the numbers may be too small to really prove anything, but I am optimistic enough to feel that some of what was achieved at Ardale was most definitely a contributory factor.

Table 11.4. This table, too, dispels another myth which states that boys from CH(E)s float from one job to another in an aimless fashion, leaving after only a short time. With both groups, very few boys had more than two jobs in the first year. Once again, the 'hard-core' group comes out slightly on top in respect to a lack of chopping and changing jobs in the early days.

Table 11.5. The information for this section was primarily obtained from the boys themselves and must, naturally, be open to some doubt. Only two of the 'hard-core' group and none of the normal group admitted to getting dismissed. It is significant that of the eighteen (combined groups) who left of their own accord, eleven said that the pay was not good enough, and six that they were bored. The other one said he did not like shift work. We had expected some of the coloured boys who left to state that there had been some racial discrimination at work, but this was not once mentioned as a reason for leaving. Still, if a coloured boy is offered a job in the first place, it is less likely that he will be discriminated against once he starts. The boys who stated that they were seeking better jobs when they left, although they all mentioned pay, said that they were seeking a job with more prospects. One coloured boy who had originally obtained a job in a factory as an assistant maintenance man stated when he visited something to the effect of: 'All I had to do was push a brush around, make tea and look busy. The women in the factory were very nice really, but one of them said that I would still be pushing a broom around when I was her age as there were no good jobs there—Christ, she must have been pushing on to forty!'

Table 11.6. This is the most significant of the five tables as far as the system of helping boys find employment goes. Most CH(E) principals maintain that a boy should not leave a CH(E) until he has somewhere to live and a job to go to. In a way, we apply stress . to the boy and the social worker by insisting on this. 89 per cent of the 'hard-core' group and 76 per cent of the normal group managed to obtain employment within a month of leaving Ardale. As the standard length of employment leave is approximately a month, this certainly indicates that the system of putting pressure on the boys to seek and obtain employment really works. This, of course, is not a special tool used with just the 'hard-core' boy, but a system built into Ardale over the past six years.

Table 11.7. There is a certain degree of compression in this table. For example, one boy obtained a job in a public library, stacking the shelves and libraries have been included with shops. The percentage of both categories going into garage or motor work was higher than expected, although a few of the boys were just petrol pump attendants. From 1975 onwards, the plumbing instructor gradually switched to motor mechanics and, when he retired, plumbing was dropped altogether. Instead we appointed a full time motor mechanics instructor. Those who obtained work in the building trades were mainly concerned with brickwork, labouring and joinery. Not one single boy from either group obtained work in the plastering trades.

Other employment with the two 'hard-core' boys consisted of one working in a betting office and one who worked as a clerical assistant in an office. As this boy had obtained two GCE passes, it was felt that he may have been seeking a post where he could use his talents but he informed us that his uncle had got him the job because he worked there as a night porter. The boy was not happy and stated that he left after about two months to seek a job with more prospects. He then went into market trading and is, to the best of our knowledge, still there.

Conclusions on the employment situation

By using the small sample group alone it is still justified to assume that the Ardale experiment was a success as far as boys obtaining employment was concerned. Obviously this is merely one of the factors for defining success, but it definitely indicates that the so-called unhelpable boys can be helped not only within the confines of a CH(E) but when they re-enter the outside world. Statistic collecting is a long and laborious business, but it is the only way of showing if the results of the experiment have proved fruitful. In the field of obtaining employment alone, there was some success.

Parental relationships and accommodation after leaving Ardale

Quite a number of the boys—'hard-core' and normal—coming into Ardale had been taken into care quite young. Of the two groups followed-up after leaving, 46 per cent of the 'hard-core' and 22 per cent of the normal group had, for varying periods, been taken into care and away from their parents by the time they were twelve years old. Being taken into care did not automatically signify that the boy was removed from home but, in over half the cases this is what really happened. In effect, some boys lost all contact with their natural parents and, in a much larger percentage than probably imagined, lost all desire to continue or re-open parental contacts.

Prior to the summer holiday period in 1978, there were eight boys it was known would be staying at Ardale. This is quite a usual figure as I often refer to Ardale like the pre-war Windmill Theatre— 'We Never Close'. Remember that in 1978, the Ardale experiment had been finished for a full two years. Of the eight boys who were not going home, three of them were boys who could have done so if they wanted. The social workers nor the parents had any real objection. It was the boys themselves who opted to stay at Ardale— with all the boredom that a two to three week holiday period can bring with the majority of the staff on holiday at the same time as the boys. Sometime during the holiday period, I asked all three boys (two white and one black) why they didn't want to go home. These are the reasons they gave:

Boy one: My old woman's always sick and expects me to fetch and carry for her all the time. I don't mind helping out, but she expects me to stay in every night. I brought my bird round one night and the old woman came downstairs and had one of her turns. Both my sisters have left home because of her and the old man pissed off years ago. I don't blame him one bit really, although he was a drunken old sod'.

Boy two: I remember the day my mother died. I was only six and my granny came in to look after me. Do you know, Sir, that the very next day, dad brought his fancy woman into the house. My gran told me that it was because my dad was always knocking about with other women that my mum died of a broken heart. I really believed her at the time too. A few weeks later, dad married Nancy but I could never get on with her. I spent most of the time with my granny until she died and I was taken into care. I sometimes see my dad when I go home, but Nancy doesn't want me living with her any more than I want to'.

Boy three: My old lady is a slag. Every time I go home she's in bed with a different bloke. Bloody hell, I've had my leg over, if you know what I mean, but she should have been born a bleeding rabbit. Even the fuzz are fucking her'.

For those of us who have had relatively stable home backgrounds, some of the above sentiments can seem hard and even cruel. Why shouldn't a son look after his sick mother? Why shouldn't a relatively young man re-marry? Why should a divorced woman live like a Victorian nun? However, there is much more to it than this.

The subject of maternal deprivation and separation has been widely written about and discussed. Even the experts like Bowlby and Rutter cannot agree on many points. Perhaps the one point that all writers on the vast subject do tend to agree on is that most disorders of conduct, personality, language, cognition and even physical growth, is usually found to occur in children with serious maternal disturbances in their early family life. It is not just deprivation either. There is a fairly high record of positive evidence to indicate that children from homes with a lot of discord and quarrelling between parents do tend to have many serious behavioural and emotional problems in later life.

The vast subject of bonds, attachments, parental substitutes, etc. is one which all residential workers should have some basic grounding in. Often overheard is a young and inexperienced social worker (residential as well as field social worker) telling a child he shouldn't speak like that about his parents. Most of them have virtually no knowledge of what it is to be an unwanted, deprived or even battered child. They have no idea of what it is like to be brought up in a series of residential establishments.

Even last century, observers like Charles Dickens were aware of the emotional problems suffered by children in institutions. Residential child care has progressed somewhat since the days of Oliver Twist, but the basic problems of child/parental feelings have hardly changed at all. Bearing this fact in mind, let us now look at those children from the Ardale experiment who opted to return to what can often be most kindly described as unsatisfactory homes.

Once again, the same two groups are used but included are the very few boys who left to return to a day school. Initially, when beginning to formulate follow-up statistics, it was not possible to include the boys who left during the course of the experiment because they were sent to Borstal or DC. However, now in late 1979, over three years since the last boy came into the experiment, and over twelve months since the last boy left who was involved in either the experiment or the sample group, it has been possible to check on the boys who returned from further custodial sentences after leaving Ardale. For the purpose, therefore, of this section, figures are based on fifty boys involved with the Ardale experiment and twenty-five boys from the random sample or normal group.

The significance of these figures, perhaps more than any others shown indicates what being in care is all about. Those well meaning folk who say that bad parents are better than no parents at all should stop and wonder what the children themselves think about it all. If all the boys in the two groups had been compelled to go to their natural parents home, the percentages would have looked much healthier. It would have been possible to state that over 80 per cent from both groups had left a CH(E) and returned home. As it is, the truth is a bit more stark and realistic.

Table 11.8

Accommodation details of school leavers

	'Hard-core'		Normal	
	No.	%	No.	%
Boys who returned to their natural home	19	38	14	56
Boys who went to live with other relations or family	11	22	2	8
Boys who lived with friends or non-family	4	8	2	8
Boys who went to hostels or similar lodgings	9	18	3	12
Boys who found other form of accommodation	2	4	0	0
No information available	5	10	4	16

There is a general and quite natural fear that children who have been in residential care for any length of time become institutionalised and cannot cope in a non-residential situation. If this were true, we would expect to find a great deal more than 15 per cent going into hostels when they left a CH(E). Once again, this is a comfortable myth which doesn't reflect very much but the fears of certain categories of people who place children in residential care and then have second thoughts! CH(E) staff have argued against this myth for a long time and stated that if it were true, far more boys would be seeking some form of continuing institutionalisation. Even the very few boys who seek to make the armed forces their career could be regarded as looking for employment where everything is done and provided for them. However, the numbers seeking to become soldiers, sailors or airmen is so small and recruitment now is so selective, that very few CH(E) boys regard the services as a viable form of employment.

The group of boys who went to live with other relations also threw up a remarkable piece of information not realised before, probably because it had never really been given much thought. Well over half this group went to live with an elder sister and gave the reason for this as getting on well with her husband. It would, according to this minor piece of research, appear that in-laws are much more tolerant and accepting than family. Naturally it would be foolish to put this finding down as a concrete fact, but it may be an area which could well stand some positive research. I would very much like to know if mine is just a coincidental finding or whether it has some deeper relevance in the field of child research.

The two boys who found other form of accommodation did so on the basis of their employment. Certain firms have their own hotels or hostels where their workers can live quite comfortably at a nominal rental. One of these is a local firm and the boy from my 'hard-core' group who initially obtained employment there was visited by Ardale staff three or four times.

Why some boys went to live at home when leaving

Being if nothing else a realist, I sometimes wondered not why so few boys returned home when they left Ardale, but why so many did. There have been cases of boys who very rarely wanted to go home for periods of leave who finally decided to return home. There have been telephone calls by the score from parents who say that they never want to see their son home again, but have made no real objection to having him when it has been time for him to leave. Although parents were rarely asked why they wanted to have their sons home after finishing their stay at Ardale, we did make a point of checking with a large number of boys who had opted to return home what their reasons were. They were asked: 'Do you love your parents/mum/dad?' Surprisingly this was often a very difficult question to answer. Here are a few replies to this apparently easy question from the 'hard-core' group:

I honestly don't know what you mean by love

No, but I've got nobody else, have I?

Yes, just about as much as they love me ...

I couldn't care less about either of them ...

In view of the above comments—and many similar—we decided to ask various groups of boys who had opted to go back home when they left just why they had made that choice. We ignored such answers as: 'My social worker says I've got to' or 'That's where you are going to send me when I leave' and pointed out that nobody was going to force any of the boys to return home if they really did not wish to go there. Having got over this attempt to blame shift, we were then able to work out some reasons and obtain some simple information. Of the nineteen 'hard-core' group who returned home, we were able to ask sixteen of them. Similarly with the fourteen normal group we discussed the matter with twelve of them. Out of curiosity, I asked the first ten boys who left in 1978 and returned home—two years later.

As can be seen by Table 11.9, the results for all three groups bear many similarities. In fact, the only real difference in any of the three sets of replies is that there appears to be a diminuation of boys who state they return home because there is nowhere else for them to go. Some of the other reasons were quite amusing really: 'My mother's a good cook', 'My dad brings me home a bottle from the pub'; but my favourite—and I'm still not sure whether or not the boy was playing me along—was 'Because out of my bedroom window I can see the bird next door getting undressed'. Once again, it must be stressed that the percentage figures shown in Table 11.9 are simply on what the boys themselves stated. The only other point to remember is the remarkable similarity spread over a period of four uears.

Table 11.9

Reasons given why boys returned to natural home

	'Hard-core'	Normal	1978 group
I want to go home	18	22	28
My parent(s) want me home	10	12	12
My parent(s) need me home	6	4	6
All my friends live near by	22	22	24
There's nowhere else to go	32	22	18
I'm going to leave home as soon as I can	6	6	0
Unwillingness to go to hostel	6	8	8
Other reasons given	0	4	4

The influence of the peer group with school-leavers

Totally ignoring all that has been written on the sub-culture of delinquent youth, the above table alone gives a clear indication of the power of the peer group. At least 22 per cent of all three groups gave their main reason for returning home as a desire to be a part of the peer group again. One or two boys mentioned girl friends, but it seems generally assumed that it does not matter if a girl friend lives some distance away, but the male peer group must be in close proximity. There has been too much written on the philosophy of 'the gang' and youth sub-cultures to comment, except to add Ardale's findings to the melting pot and agree that the neighbourhood peer group—whether intent on mischief or not—appears to be a very strong reason for a boy wishing to return home and by far exceeds any maternal or paternal pull home may have. This is as equally prevalent with coloured as white boys, despite the fear of getting picked up on 'sus' when any group of coloured boys congregate in certain areas of London.

Other general information about the 'hard-core' school leaver

Once again, I have to attempt to destroy another myth about young people. The popular cry from such excellent people as Lord Baden-Powell was that youth organisations take boys from off the streets and channel their high spirits into something productive. Even the Duke of Edinburgh uses this same approach for his award scheme. Let us take a slightly closer look at this hypothesis.

In theory, there is supposed to be no real class barrier, apart from that of being born into the aristocracy or into a very wealthy household, in this country. This is untrue. There is just as much a class barrier now as there ever was but some adults try to pretend it is not there—especially those aspiring to move up in the world. Teenagers have a far more realistic view of life and know that there are some things they can do and some things they are not really accepted into. Most of the youth movements do not go out of their way to actively encourage membership from boys or girls who have been in trouble. There is the well meaning philanthropist scout master or cadet officer who feels he is being public spirited by taking in a small percentage of delinquent children—but look closely how small the percentage is or listen to the patronising way these kids are received and it does not take long to realise why so many national youth movements are almost taboo for CH(E) and ex-CH(E) boys. The same attitude appears to continue into later life.

Therefore, to regard membership of organisations as being a criteria of success needs explaining. There are one or two boys who during the course of their stay or shortly after leaving a CH(E) 'get religion'. This usually means that they have come into contact with somebody—quite frequently a girl friend—who practices some form of religious ceremony and regularly attends religious functions. If a boy genuinely joins such a religious group, it is fairly safe to say that he is in the best possible organisation for helping him. Many converts are given genuine help. Let me not try to pretend that boys rush out of Ardale to become monks—all I am trying to say is that if a boy joins a religious group, he is usually helped to come to terms with himself and society much more actively than if he were to join a national youth movement.

The majority of boys leaving CH(E)s who decide to join organised groups do so for a number of quite basic reasons:

1 To meet the opposite sex.
2 To be part of the gang.

138

3 To relax without too many adult pressures.
4 To play such games as table tennis, etc. which are not available in their own homes.
5 As a form of escapism from boredom.
6 To enjoy their own type of music.
7 For nefarious and criminal reasons.

Any one or a combination of any of the above will adequately explain why discos are much more popular than social service youth clubs. In item 7 drink and drugs which may be openly or secretly passed around are included.

The majority of organisations which provide any of the above, apart from perhaps 4, are almost always run by private or non-social work bodies. Voluntary youth clubs with a bouncer-type superviser tend to be much more popular with ex-Ardale boys than what they generally class as the more namby-pamby type of youth club. Music must be loud, there must be the correct mix of male/female, and they must be allowed to show off without too many restrictions on their attitude. However, there must always be a figure of authority who hurls people out if they are too outrageous!!

Virtually the whole of the last sentence was stated by one of the 'hard-core' boys shortly before he left when he was discussing what he was going to do with his spare time. In view of this, it was found impossible to formulate statistical tables about membership of clubs, as the boys tended not to regard certain weekly or even regular evening activities, such as discos, as clubs. What was found was that not one single boy from the 'hard-core' group and only two from the normal sample group mentioned at any time that they had ever gone to what is usually referred to as a youth club.

Sexual relationships

One of the most significant factors with any teenage boy is that of having a regular girl friend. There appears to be few more positive factors in helping a boy fit back into society than having a girl friend who admires, respects and encourages him. It is difficult to define what a steady girl friend means, so we have gone back to the easiest classification of all—length of time a boy has been going out with her. Of the fifty boys from the 'hard-core' group and the twenty-five from the normal group, we were able to discuss this with only twenty-three and eleven respectively. This is what was learned from the boys, and in certain cases the boys with their girl friends present:

139

Table 11.10

Length of courtship

	'Hard-core' 23 boys	Normal 11 boys
Regular girl friend for at least three months	14	5
Regular girl friend until recently	6	3
No regular girl friend	3	3

With some of the boys many personal questions were asked, and a number stated that their girl friends wanted to get married. Within the first year of checking after any boy left from either group, all the boys had remained single. One or two have got married since however and still visit. To the best of my knowledge, none of the six boys who indicated that they did not have current or steady girl friends, showed any indication of being homosexual. Two of them said they were not interested in the opposite sex, but this was probably not true and was just a defence mechanism to account to themselves why they had so far not struck it lucky.

General summary of follow-up research

Based purely and simply on the criteria for success, it appears that the 'hard-core' group were not only as successful as the comparison group, but in many cases more so. Despite popular mythology, they did not contribute any more greatly to the criminal statistics than any other boy leaving a CH(E). Their relationships with parents and eventual return home shows no more significant factors than any other CH(E) boy. All in all, they seem to mix better with their peers in unorganised clubs and with regular girl friends. In effect, their success is generally shown as being just above the average for boys leaving Ardale.

If one merely took the statistics for all boys leaving Ardale in between 1975-78 without any check on their pre-admission statistics nothing really relevant would stand out. This proves one of two things only: either each and every one of them was badly assessed and their previous residential behaviour was grossly exaggerated; or the special treatment of control and care given to them at Ardale gave them at least an equal opportunity as their peers.

Without any hesitation, I claim some success for my staff, and our experimental system in helping the unhelpable boy to adjust back into society by combining common sense, genuine care, and the imposition of rules and boundaries.

12 Some possible alternatives to CH(E)s for the 'hard-core' delinquent

There is a general misconception amongst many social service departments that those who work in CH(E)s are totally opposed by anything which could be regarded as an alternative resource in child care. Admittedly we are very cautious in coming out too openly in favour of many schemes which are seen as means of getting child care on the cheap. The ever rising cost of residential placements forces many heads of social service departments to seek something cheaper, well knowing that what they obtain is inferior to a good residential placement.

Before analysing the results of the Ardale experiment and discussing its implications for residential child care, it is necessary and worth while to digress slightly and look at some of the alternatives to CH(E)s. What too many of us who work in residential establishments ignore is that there are a number of children who enter CH(E)s as a last resource and, if they had been helped earlier, there would probably have been no need to accommodate them at all. Unless the present penal system is radically altered, there will always be a need for establishments similar to CH(E)s but whether or not so many are needed will be discussed in the final chapter.

Earlier I gave a very brief potted history of British child care over the past 150 years, and the gradual change in our society with regard to the ways young offenders are punished and treated. In the reign of Queen Victoria alone there were 109 acts passed specifically dealing with the care and general welfare of children. Seen, then, in this context, the 1969 Act merely represented a further stage in the evolution of a less destructive and more humane way of managing juvenile delinquents. It introduced the concept of treatment and therapy. In many respects this was a sensible approach, but like all acts of parliament, once let loose amongst the masses, many of the original concepts were altered to suit the particular ideas and ideals of a few well meaning but often quite misguided people.

The words treatment and therapy have been so bandied about for the past decade that they have become meaningless purely because they have been given so many different meanings. When talking about residential child care alone, there are so many variations that I have entitled this section as possible alternatives to CH(E)s and not alternatives to residential child care. Even the concept of what residential

141

care is appears no longer to be straight forward. In an article in *Social Work Today,* April 1978, Norman Tutt attempts to define the difference between residential and institutional care. He asks: 'When does a residential establishment (home) become an institution?':

> Obviously a child placed singly in a foster home is not in an institution, but is resident, but what about a group home with 5 children and 4 staff, or 15 children and 10 staff or 120 children and 70 staff?

Dr Tutt feels that it is essential to sort out our basic terminology. The general feeling one gets is that he is not opposed to residential care provided each child receives individual treatment—there's that word again—and is not institutionalised.

A guest speaker at the Annual Conference of Community Home Schools in 1978 put the fears of many CH(E) staff into clear perspective when she stated:

> Those who criticise residential service are often ill informed or worse still, misinformed as to what goes on there. In addition, the residential workers I know are suspicious of academics and politicians who seem to think that fostering or intermediate treatment or day care or any of the proposed forms of non-residential intervention will succeed in curing or containing delinquency and in saving money. In their eyes what we are witnessing is yet another change in the tide of public opinion which is not founded on knowledge or facts but is just a trendy gimmick. Given such an outlook, it is not at all surprising that residential child care staff are inclined to adopt a cautious let's wait and see attitude in the belief that time is on their side.

The majority of this work is concerned with one small experiment in just one CH(E). It looks closely at the whole thesis of care and control, but it is necessary to look at just a few of the viable alternatives. A brief summary is made of two residential types of training which are most decidedly alternatives to CH(E)s dealing with the 'hard-core' child, i.e. youth treatment centres and secure and intensive care units. Still remaining within the residential sphere, a brief look is taken of therapeutic communities and co-educational CH(E)s. This will be followed by three activities which could be quite logically defined as genuine alternatives in some cases: community service orders; CSV work with delinquent youth; intermediate treatment, including the scheme which until recently was run at Ardale. There are no apologies for ignoring fostering as my personal feeling is that very few indeed of the boys who come under the classification of 'hard-core' are likely to be willingly accepted for fostering, despite the financial incentive in certain schemes.

Youth treatment centres

> The Youth Treatment Centre will provide long term care and
> treatment for a small minority of severely disturbed and anti-
> social adolescent boys and girls whose specialised treatment
> needs cannot satisfactorily be met in any existing forms of
> residential provision: boys and girls whose problems are so
> complex and whose behaviour is so disruptive and disturbed
> that neither children's homes, nor approved schools (soon to
> become community homes), nor hospitals, nor special schools,
> have the total facilities (including the need for physical secur-
> ity) needed to provide them with the long term care, control
> and treatment that their condition requires. (HMSO, 1971)

Less than a decade ago, the first secure unit for highly disturbed
children began to admit such boys and girls. This was a youth
treatment centre situated only twelve miles from Ardale. Since then,
one in Birmingham and another in Wakefield have opened their
doors.

I have been in contact with the Essex one from the start. No bars
or any form of physical barrier are obvious, although from the back
can be seen a high wall surrounding one particular area. The unit is
designed to admit a total of thirty-six children, but usually keeps
slightly under that figure.

Unlike all approved schools and most CH(E)s, youth treatment
centres admit boys and girls, and the treatment is long term. Most
of the children are between the ages of twelve and sixteen, although
the length of the programme sometimes necessitates this being altered
slightly. The staff, who come from many different professions—medical, educational, social work, etc.—are all referred to as group workers
and basically share many of the same day to day tasks with each
other.

Any success is considerably based on the highly qualified and
carefully selected staff and the very high ratio of staff to children.
The centre is divided into three units or houses, each with at least
a dozen group workers and, in some cases, considerably more. When
a child arrives, following a referral by the DHSS and a complicated
pre-admission process, he is allocated an individual counsellor, called
a host worker. It is this specific member of staff who will have
visited the child at home prior to admission.

An integral part of the treatment programme is on-going work
with the families of the children. They are strongly encouraged to

143

involve themselves with what takes place at the centre, and when children eventually make a visit home this is done in progressive stages—first as a visit with a member of staff, then a sole visit, then an overnight stay or a weekend pass. As with boys in CH(E)s, visits home are not always beneficial at first, but they must be persevered with.

The Essex YTC still uses the word treatment almost exclusively and bases this on a therapeutic model. The children live in a specially created secure environment where close studies are made of maturation, growth, achievement and positive functioning. The forming of good relationships is seen as being of prime importance. With a battery of specialists at hand, there is always the availability to use group therapy, psychotherapy, psychodrama, and basic behaviour modification techniques.

The initial concept of security is soon relaxed with most children and many of them are allowed to go shopping in the nearby town.

Like any form of residential treatment resource, but more so with the vast expense of a YTC place, they have their successes and their failures. Like CH(E)s they occasionally hit the headlines about wasting public expenditure, etc.

From my knowledge of the work being carried out at the Essex YTC it is obvious that (a) they most certainly do provide positive help to a certain category of the most disturbed type of teenager in this country: and (b) there are not enough of them. The latter point can be quite frustrating for heads of CH(E)s who feel that they have a child who could be much better helped in a YTC There are so few places available that it may be worth thinking about if I mention that perhaps one or two of the present and conventional CH(E)s could be made into YTCs. However, this will be discussed further in the concluding chapter.

Secure and intensive care units

> The psychological consequences of a period in security do not seem deleterious, at least in the short term. While these advantages should not be underestimated, the rapid return to custody of the majority of boys released provides little comfort. Security offers an expensive and very short respite from the age old problems presented by high risk boys. It certainly offers no solution. (Millham, et al., 1978)

Thus concludes Millham et al in *Locking Up Children*. Let us take a closer look at what locking up our children really means.

The headmaster of the first secure unit ever founded—at Kingswood

School in Bristol states: 'The first definition of 'secure' that I came across in the dictionary was 'free from care'. It would not be difficult to conclude from this that where there is security there is no care'. There appears to be a great deal of support for this idea, particularly when it is children who are locked up.

Society has most definite mixed approaches to the use of any form of secure accommodation. Imprisonment has been in use as a form of punishment for over a thousand years. It is, therefore, quite natural that many people will regard a secure or intensive care unit as a children's prison. One has only to look at the way we cared for our mentally sick until recently by treating them the same—and often a good deal worse—as our criminals. Recently the topic of security for children in care has become a focal point again, and many opinions are quoted for and against.

There are two main types of secure facility which social services have responsibility for. One is the secure unit, which can be part of a CH(E) or RAC. These units usually consist of a suite of rooms and allow for comfortable living and educational facilities within a secure boundary. Staffing ratios are high. The other form of secure accommodation is the single separation room, still common in many former remand homes, and quite often still being planned in new assessment centres. Let us, for a moment look at what a separation room can offer and what it removes.

The main use of a separation room is threefold:

1 To hold absconders, children who have been apprehended as absconders or potential absconders.
2 To remove a child for a short period who is a positive danger to other children or staff.
3 To temporarily contain the acting-out boy who may be in danger of damaging himself.

The initial one could be regarded as a functional reason—somewhere to put a boy who has been arrested late at night, or a newly admitted boy who has made it quite clear that he is going to abscond at the very first opportunity. This reason, perhaps more than the other two comes in for the majority of criticism *viz a viz* penal type treatment. The latter two can be termed therapeutic reasons. In other words it is possible for positive treatment concepts such as counselling and therapy to be used on a one-to-one basis in security which would not be available without it. Often the only way to get a child to accept his situation and to face up to his problems is by withdrawing him from the group.

The deleterious aspect, as with almost all forms of locking a person (child or adult) away, even for short periods are deprivation of liberty and choice, lack or diminuation of educational and recreational facilities, a breakdown in roles, and the personal antagonism such a person feels by being singled out from the group. All these problems are very real ones and it is necessary when thinking of creating a separation room, to think more of the number, quality and attitudes of the staff administering them than it is on whether or not to have bars on the window or double locks on the doors.

A secure unit is quite different from a separation room, although many of the basic problems are the same. This is almost invariably a much longer termed form of treatment than the temporary use of a special room. A good number have been built and more are being planned. There is considerable controversy on the actual design of such units, but the general consensus of opinion is that each should provide an environment in which the children—and staff running them—should be safe, secure, well looked after; a place where basic needs can be met and relationships formed and shared. As much as anything, a secure unit should give a boy a chance to make a new beginning away from all external pressures, where he can be guided to take a close look at himself and his attitudes.

Obviously this is an ideal situation with ideal boys and ideal staff. We are all too painfully aware though that ideal situations do not exist very often. There are problems in dealing with children in security and in some cases the good work is outweighed by the mere problems automatically thrown up by any form of incarceration. Nobody who has visited one or spent some time at one will say that a secure unit is ideal for every child passing through the CH(E) system.

As with youth treatment centres, there are still very few places available and many boys who could perhaps receive some positive help by being admitted must remain in CH(E)s. Let nobody deny however that security has advantages for some children.

Therapeutic communities

One wonders if there is any such thing as a therapeutic community outside of a clinical setting. It is a phrase used to define a concept rather than a reality. There are, however, a number of establishments, including ex-approved schools which have made great strides towards creating a different atmosphere and ethos to the more conventional CH(E). There are probably more misconceptions about therapeutic communities than there are about secure care. Many people still think that they are run by a lot of idealists who let the kids do as they please when they please. In effect, just the opposite is true and there are probably more boundaries than in many CH(E)s. There must be a fairly large and well experienced staff who are capable of allowing boys to progress at their own individual speed while at the same time ensuring that they are working to their full potential. Group work plays a considerable role, sometimes conducted by specialists and at other times by staff members and the boys themselves.

One of the criticisms of CH(E)s is that they tend to deal with the boy, more often than not, in isolation from his family. In a TC, family therapy is of prime importance. This, of course, has a side issue. The selection procedure for admission to a TC is very intense and many boys are not accepted. It is usual to insist from the start that the family involves itself: if this is not agreed to, a number of the boys are not admitted as it is felt that without the total support of the family, no real therapeutic progress can be made. Obviously, many of these rejectees then come to a CH(E) and it is not likely that they are going to get any more parental support than the TC and usually a good deal less. The selection criteria, especially the one in which very few boys of below average intelligence are admitted, has, in the past, caused a certain amount of criticism from CH(E) heads who sometimes feel that the claimed success rate is with the cream, while those boys rejected as likely not to benefit from the system filter into the CH(E) system. This may be true or not and could be very unfair on those staff who are working in therapeutic communities.

The biggest advantage a TC has over a CH(E) is that the system forces a boy to look at himself and eventually discuss his problems with his peers as well as the staff. All who work in CH(E)s know how easy it is for certain boys to be seen to be conforming, who cause no management problems, but really are using their conformity like a shield to avoid all relationships with adults or peers other than those necessary for basic survival. Many staff in CH(E)s are not capable of living in a situation of being tested-out almost every working hour. This is quite often the norm in a TC.

Ever since August Aichorn wrote *Wayward Youth* many years ago there has been continual argument about the use of regression techniques in both a medical and an educational context. Too many people imagine that it is necessary or even generally possible to regress a difficult teenager back to the 'potty stage'. In the main, a TC uses regression techniques based on the criteria that each boy, at his own speed may need to slightly regress before he can mature. This is carried out by skilled practitioners and is not a tool staff can normally use in a CH(E).

It would appear, then, that for a certain type of child, the daily regime in a therapeutic community has many positive advantages

147

over the conventional regime of a CH(E). Within the limits they have set themselves and by a very strict selection process, it is obvious that certain children who fall into the 'hard-core' category due to extreme emotional disturbance could be helped by a properly run and organised therapeutic community. They cannot, in the main, deal with the extremely violent boy, but they do have positive advantages for the boy who is able to become part of a group and able to withstand and benefit from the pressures such groups put upon him.

Co-educational CH(E)s

The development of co-educational CH(E)s is, in many respects, a surprising and mushrooming growth. The approved school system would never accept it and, even today, many residential child care staff are hesitant in treating disturbed boys and girls together, especially with the age range of child normally dealt with. Excluding the theory that teenage boys and girls living together in a CH(E) will be in a perpetual state of promiscuity, it is worth looking at some of the possible advantages and disadvantages.

These are really quite simple—superficially at least. If residential life is to correlate to life outside, it is unnatural to segragate the sexes. Many children coming into CH(E)s have brothers and sisters: to suddenly remove them to a one sexed society could be regarded as damaging to their emotional growth. There is still a tendency for most boys CH(E)s to be predominantly staffed by men and for most girls CH(E)s to be mainly staffed by women. This further aggravates the system of sexual segregation. Most of the children coming into CH(E)s have received normal schooling in a co-educational setting. Most of the children in CH(E)s will eventually marry and have children of their own. Nobody knows if early sexual segregation has an adverse factor in this respect. Many of the boys coming into CH(E)s need positive female support: must this always be from the staff or could not a mixed peer group provide some of this? Normal competition and rivalry between the sexes is a natural and healthy state, often having considerable advantages.

Looking at the obverse side of the coin; is that girls and boys in CH(E)s often have very different problems which need quite different approaches which badly combine together. It can be stated that a male particularly needs some period of his life to live in a masculine society—the forces, male clubs, etc. The considerable expense needed to adapt a one sexed CH(E) to a mixed sexed one is often prohibitive. Even in the last quarter of the twentieth century it is not standard practice to combine the boys and girls sleeping quarters. Let them work, play and eat together, but there must be separate, and usually well separated, sleeping quarters. Mention will be made in the final section of the possibilities of Ardale going co-educational should this ever be agreed to be a topic of genuine discussion. It is not possible to merely say that one of the four house units will admit girls and to leave it at that. Unfortunately, some of the earlier pioneers did work on a shoe string budget and it is great credit to these early pioneers that certain CH(E)s did make a success, after a very shaky start, of going co-educational.

In the early 1960s, a Home Office report, based on the findings of a research unit considered that there was no evidence to show delinquent youngsters could benefit any more from a mixed approved school than a single sex school. In 1969, a questionnaire was sent to staff in approved schools asking their views. Much later an evaluation of the replies was circulated to those who had taken part:

1 The majority of approved school staff were in favour of co-education in the state school system (78 per cent).
2 A large proportion of staff who were educated in single-sex schools showed a preference for co-education (84 per cent).
3 Almost all the staff who had been educated in a co-educational school were happy, fairly happy or very happy at their school (92 per cent).
4 The majority of the teaching staff in approved schools preferred co-education in normal state school education (88 per cent).
5 Over 75 per cent of approved school staff were in favour of mixing delinquent boys and girls in the same establishment. Only 14 per cent were totally opposed to the idea.

The findings of the questionnaire administered were, naturally, very limited. Some replies may have been influenced by the fact that the idea of co-education for delinquents in this country was becoming the in-thing and it could have been fashionable to support the notion. Nevertheless, despite its limitations, the survey showed that the majority of those responsible for the care and education of delinquent boys and girls favoured co-education.

Whether or not certain categories of those boys classified as 'hard-core' would benefit from co-education remains to be seen. Personally I feel that some of them would, but one would obviously have to be extra selective.

Community service orders

The main problem with CSOs, as far as CH(E)s are concerned is that the minimum age is seventeen, although this could perhaps be reduced by a year.

Community service by offenders originated with a recommendation in the Wootton Committee Report of 1970, which looked for ways of countering the rising prison and Borstal population by new forms of treatment. In general terms the committee's proposal was that the courts should be given power to order offenders to carry out a specified number of hours' work for the community in their spare time and that this should be oversighted by the probation department. Perhaps somewhat similar to the attendance centre order, but with far more teeth and relevance. The recommendation became law by the Criminal Justice Act of 1972 and was consolidated by the Powers of Criminal Courts Act in 1973.

With all legal statutes, certain criteria must be met before a court can issue a community service order. Apart from the age limit, an offender must have been convicted for an offence normally warranting imprisonment and he must agree to fully carrying out any such work given him by the court or his probation officer. A court can award not less than forty and no more than 240 hours of community service.

A main feature of the work is that it is completely unpaid and is normally that carried out by a voluntary agency such as decorating old people's flats, building adventure playgrounds, teaching handicapped children to swim, or helping at disabled people's sports clubs. These are but a few of the various tasks which can be undertaken. It is unique amongst penal sentences in that it not only takes away an offender's personal leisure time but puts him—probably for the first time in his life—in a position of helping people who are often much worse off than himself.

Obviously the lower age limit of seventeen makes it an inappropriate alternative to a CH(E) for all but a very few boys. I would like to suggest that some further research be carried out to study the possibility of lowering the age from seventeen to sixteen or even fifteen. There are a few boys at present in CH(E)s who may perhaps have never needed a residential placement if they had been compelled by law to give up their leisure time to helping others. It could now be the appropriate time to combine attendance centre orders with community service orders and come up with something which has the attributes of both.

Community service volunteers - children in care programme

Community service volunteers (known world wide as CSV) launched its 'Children In Care' programme in September 1973. This programme, funded by the DHSS, was established to foster and organise the involvement of children in care in 'service' to the community. The initial stages of the programme were monitored by an advisory group consisting of a triumvirate of Dr N. Tutt, Principal Social Work Services Officer for the DHSS, Mr P. Friend, superintendent of a large reception home, and myself, principal of Ardale CH(E). Before the programme got off the ground, careful consideration was given to the special needs of children in care becoming CSVs, but it was not designed exclusively for such children.

Children in CH(E)s, as in any other group, present a diversity of skills and interests which can be mobilised for the benefit of others. This caring potential has been noted from way back into the early days of approved schools. Frequently those who work in CH(E)s have observed how boys respond in a naturally sensitive and helpful way to the needs of other children, especially those younger than themselves. All of us who have brought up our families in CH(E) and approved school settings know what a good relationship can be formed between our own children and those in the school. Encouragement is given to staff to let their own children mix with the boys at Ardale until the staff children themselves feel they no longer want to.

Since 1973, Ardale has rarely been without a couple of CSVs who work with the boys in the local community. In 1976, Ardale won the Shell Community Service Award for some of its activities which included, amongst many others:

1 Designing, making and erecting sixteen boundary stones for the local council.
2 Designing and constructing an adventure playground for a group of mentally handicapped children.
3 Carrying out a reading project at a local primary school.
4 Football coaching at another local primary school.
5 Taking patients to discos, filmshows etc. at a local mental subnormality hospital.
6 Constructing and repairing playground equipment for a local training centre.
7 Gardening and grass cutting for the local old folk.

A few of the boys became so engrossed with the work they had carried out with the assistance and guidance of CSVs who worked at Ardale, that they opted to become full time CSVs when they left. Up to the end of 1978, over 100 young people from various

CH(E)s and other community homes have worked or are at present working as full time CSVs in a wide variety of caring situations. Most are between the ages of fifteen and seventeen and a half, most are on care orders, and many are sponsored directly by social workers. Young people on social work caseloads represent an enormous potential resource and could be of great value, to others as well as themselves particularly at a time when all agencies are having to watch their spending.

Some of the hardest of the 'hard-core' category really benefited from working with others in the local community. Naturally, other schools in the locality have caught on to the idea and copied the example set by Ardale, and so frequently published and discussed in the local press. New opportunities are getting hard to find but it has been a proven tool in helping severly damaged delinquents to realise that there are many others much worse off than themselves.

Intermediate treatment

So much has been written recently about this alternative to residential treatment that this section merely discusses how a CH(E) and a local authority IT scheme can pool their resources and work together.

My interest in intermediate treatment was not something new and I never saw it as a threat to CH(E)s, despite the spate of publicity stating how it could be not only much more successful but also much cheaper. In early 1974 I was invited to join Newham Social Service Department's Intermediate Treatment Panel. Our aims were fourfold:

1 To give advice to social workers regarding the facilities available to them; in this respect social workers who wished to bring a case to the meeting for discussion were always welcome.
2 To form an alliance with the governing boroughs and the Essex Magistrate's Association.
3 To evaluate the on-going needs of the area and develop new ideas for submission to the Regional Planning Committee.
4 To conduct a limited amount of research into the effectiveness of intermediate treatment.

In full agreement with the Director of Social Services and the head of the Residential Services Division at Newham, I offered the Panel and any social worker interested in taking up the offer, certain facilities at Ardale. These included the use of a large four bedroomed house, camping facilities, the use of the gym, woods, swimming pool, tennis court, etc. During the summer holidays of 1974, we held our first residential IT week with a group of boys ranging from nine to fifteen.

Some of the lessons we learned were the need for a far greater boy/staff ratio, the need to have a much smaller age range gap, and the positive value the boys from Ardale could play not just in erecting tents but actually working with the boys on IT. Shortly after this camp we held a weekend training seminar in IT in which a number of social workers, probation officers, youth workers, and staff and certain boys from Ardale were present.

IT activities blossomed at Ardale for some considerable time, and many of the 'hard-core' boys became involved. Two of them actually acted as supervisors in co-operation with a couple of police cadets for one weekend. It was quite an experience for them to be on the other side for a while. Recently, intermediate treatment in Newham has branched out into many other interesting and diverse activities. Ardale's facilities are no longer in such big demand.

A good policy of IT can, then, be a definite alternative for some children, although there are still many who will gain little benefit from it, regarding it all as a game. The best policy for CH(E)s is to accept that IT has come to stay and that it will have its successes and its failures. If we have to live with it, let us not pretend that it does not exist, but make some positive use, by working with the organisors, and actively encouraging them to allow CH(E) boys to take part side by side with boys on intermediate treatment orders.

Conclusion on alternatives to CH(E) placements

This chapter has attempted to take a very brief glance at just a few alternative ways of treating 'hard-core' delinquents. It is highly unlikely that what has been written will create much positive action and is certainly highly unlikely to reduce the number of CH(E) placements required. Many alternative placements, such as youth treatment centres and secure accommodation are so scarce that the majority of highly disturbed delinquents will still come through the CH(E) system. The failures of intermediate treatment schemes are already trickling into CH(E)s, and nobody should expect any scheme which deals with disturbed adolescents not to have failures whether it be residential or community based.

Two factors are running side by side at the moment—there is a continual increase in violent crime amongst teenagers, and the cost of residential placements is rapidly escalating. Crime figures for some London areas published in September 1978, show that robberies and violent thefts have doubled and, in some cases trebled, during the first six months of 1978 compared with a similar period in 1977.

There appears to be a change in public attitude towards crime, especially crimes of violence. The pendulum is swinging back to a more controlled form of dealing with young offenders. The therapeutic approach, stemming from the 1969 Children and Young Persons Act, seems to have almost run its course and no longer does everybody try to convince themselves that all forms of delinquency can be treated within the community.

Most experienced residential workers are fully aware that the therapeutic concept, despite all its advantages, was taken to excess in many cases. Will we now see the reverse happen? Whatever method is used to help young delinquents of the 'hard-core' variety, there needs to be just the right mix of care and control. It is when one takes the leading role over the other that serious, and often dangerous problems arise.

13   Recent developments at Ardale

The initial effects of the 'Ardale experiment'

In Autumn 1976, the results and consequences of the 'hard-core'
experiment were discussed in detail at an Ardale management sub-
committee. Obviously, only a few basic facts were then known about
what had happened to the boys in the experiment after they had
left Ardale. I had published these facts and figures earlier in the
Community Homes Schools Gazette. What was known, however, was
the considerable apprehension some of the staff had about continuing the scheme; not, it should be noted, the staff who had been
mainly responsible for running it. The number of West Indian boys
had increased and some staff were talking about a black take-over
bid. By now most of the staff were aware that Ardale had been
admitting boys who, in the main, had been refused a place at
other CH(E)s. There was slowly beginning to form a nucleus of staff
whose morale was sinking and who were regularly complaining that
the experiment should cease. Like any lowering of morale, this
gradually began to spread, particularly with members of staff who
had been appointed after the scheme began.

It would have been possible to ignore this and soldier on, but if
the scheme was to succeed, it must have the support of at least 75
per cent of the staff. When it was felt that those supporting it had
dropped below this figure, it was discussed in considerable detail
with the head of the residential services division and the principal
adviser (residential) from Newham's Social Services Department. I
was advised to put it in my report to the managers' meeting, which
I did.

The outcome of this meeting was, therefore, quite predictable.
Although it was fully agreed that all evidence seemed to indicate
that the experiment was highly successful as far as the boys involved
were concerned, it was felt that:

1 Ardale was being too liberal in admitting boys whom other
CH(E)s were constantly refusing to take.
2 The experiment was having an adverse effect on many of the
staff and lowering morale.
3 It was possible that some of the other boys were suffering
from the behaviour of the 'hard-core' group.

4 Although a few boys had obviously gained considerable benefit, the staffing ratios at Ardale were just not high enough to justify its continuation.

Accordingly, I was informed that I should cease the scheme. As we had already agreed to accept two more boys of the 'hard-core' definition it was felt that these should be admitted but no more.

Non-Ardale matters effecting future development

The DHSS and the various regional planning committees, especially region eight (that dealing primarily with the London boroughs) felt in early 1976 that there was a need to look closely at CH(E)s and try to formulate some basic common policies on such matters as management, admission procedures, staffing ratios, etc.

The heads of CH(E)s which dealt mainly with London children were invited to take part in what was known as the 'Criteria Exercise'. There were many controversial points in this scheme, but in the main, we heads agreed that most of them made sense, even though it could cause many problems in organising them. The directors of social service departments for the various London boroughs, many of whom were getting considerably worried about the increasing expense of CH(E)s and the apparent refusal by some social workers to recommend a CH(E) placement, were, in the main quite enthusiastic. The Association of Directors of Social Services for the London Boroughs, chaired by the regional planning committee, invited a selected group from the South East CH(E) Heads Association to meet with them and discuss the various points. Three of my colleagues and I did just this. Although there were many minor points we could not come to a total agreement on, e.g. how long a boy should be at a CH(E) before he is allowed home leave, all the major points were felt by both directors and principals of CH(E)s to be valid.

Eventually all the evidence was correlated and the DHSS produced in late 1976 (revised in 1977) a document entitled *Management of Community Homes With Education on the Premises*—because of it's colour, known by everybody concerned as the red booklet.

Many valid points were discussed in this booklet, which quickly circulated up and down the country, even though it was primarily designed only for London based CH(E)s. As far as Ardale was concerned, the most significant was the need for each director to liaise closely with the senior staff of his CH(E) and to examine staffing levels and the boy/staff ratio in CH(E)s.

Shortly after the production of the red booklet, Newham's Director of Social Services spent a whole day at Ardale, along with

156

his senior officers from the residential services division, discussing the implications of the booklet's findings. It was agreed that the Ardale Sub-Management Committee should cease to exist forthwith and an advert be promulgated for a Principal Professional Assistant whose prime responsibilities would be to the three regional establishments in Newham—Ardale and the two regional assessment centres, Little Heath and Luton House, the latter being newly opened.

A survey of the staffing situation at Ardale

Following the decision to appoint a PPA, almost a full year elapsed before he took up his post. However, during that year many things happened. At his meeting with us, the director decided that we must hold a full survey of the staffing situation at Ardale and decided to form a committee which later became known as The Ardale Development Committee, under the chairmanship of the Head of the Residential Services Division, who shortly afterwards was promoted to Deputy Director of Social Services for Newham.

The Committee initially consisted of the Deputy Director, two officers from the London Boroughs Children's Regional Planning Committee, one representative from DHSS, two officers from Newham's Management Services Division, myself and my two deputies. Later, this group was enlarged and the Assistant Director (Children's Services) and the Principal Personnel Officer from Newham Social Services were made members of the group. Towards the end, when the PPA took up his post, he too, naturally, became a member. Apart from two meetings held in the social services department, all the remainder of the regular monthly meetings were held at Ardale.

Ardale was asked to prepare a document for the first meeting outlining what we thought were the priorities. Not only was this discussed with my two deputies, but a special staff meeting was held to let all staff know what was being discussed. Initially there was considerable scepticism, and a number of the staff thought that we may talk as long as we liked, but nothing was likely to happen. Luckily, the vast majority were extremely enthusiastic from the start.

What we felt was needed at Ardale

Prior to the first meeting of the Ardale Development Committee in October 1977, many points had been discussed and rejected. The only two points in which there was any real controversy between

Ardale's staff was the possibility of considering going co-educational and the need for some secure accommodation. As it transpired, the Committee felt that both these were matters which should possibly be discussed at a later date. They have not appeared on the agenda since then.

Following my discussions with staff, we therefore presented a list of priorities as we saw them:

1   The need to reduce the maximum number of boys from 100.
2   The need to considerably increase the staff.
3   The need to re-grade the staff.
4   The need to form a group of specialists.
5   The need to look at the feminine role at Ardale.
6   The educational specialisation should be considered.
7   The need to create positive ideas, philosophies and typologies of boys we could best help at Ardale.
8   The possible creation of a fifth or secure unit.
9   The need to modify, modernise and re-equip the boys' house units in line with the proposed philosophies.
10   The need to increase staff accommodation and to centralise senior and administration personnel.

Naturally, there were many other points and suggestions which transpired during the various meetings but, in the main, these were the ten most salient points. Points one, two and seven were the three most important and were indivisible. Without reducing the number of boys and increasing the boy/staff ratio, it would be virtually impossible to create and put into practice new philosophies of child care. The Committee agreed with this and the initial meetings were primarily concerned with what the number should be reduced to and by how many and what type of residential staff the increase should be.

The numerical decrease of boys

Ardale, being an ex-approved school, still comes under the purview of the Joint Negotiating Committee for Former Approved Schools and Remand Homes. This was insisted upon and agreed when approved schools became CH(E)s so that no staff working in them would suffer by re-organisation. Ardale, admitting up to 100 boys, was classed for all purposes as a Group Four CH(E). This quite clearly delineated staffing structures, salaries and conditions of service.

Before any reduction in numbers was considered, it had to be fully agreed that no present staff would suffer in any way if Ardale's numbers were so decreased that it became a Group Three School. Nobody would have been happy in greatly increasing child care at Ardale by reducing staff care. This was fully agreed and, when the final number of a maximum of sixty boys was agreed as Ardale's established number, no present staff would lose any of their previous conditions of service.

At the second meeting, then, of the Ardale Development Committee, it was agreed not only to reduce the number of boys from 100 to sixty, but to start a gradual process of numerically running well below sixty so that when the new system came into operation in 1979, very few of the original boys would still be at Ardale. None of us felt that it would be good child care to temporarily close Ardale and make arrangements to have the boys transferred to other CH(E)s. Accordingly, from June 1978, Ardale ceased to admit any new boys, ran down to less than twenty boys, and only began to re-admit boys in March 1979.

The increase in staff at Ardale

At the beginning of chapter 3, a few basic facts about Ardale as it was during the whole process of the 'hard-core' experiment are given. Included in this is a list of staffing. For the purpose of this section only maintenance, grounds and domestic staff, the latter which also had a proportionate increase, are ignored. From 1973 until late 1978, the Ardale professional staff consisted of:

Principal
2 deputy principals
10 teachers/instructors
4 house wardens
Matron
Assistant matron
8 housemasters
4 housemothers
Social caseworker (until 1976)
4 night supervisors (3 full time and 1 part-time)
Senior administration officer
2 clerical staff

Remember that this was for a maximum of 100 boys, and there were frequently over ninety-five on the school role.

The new staffing ratio, after much research work by the Management Services, and visits to a number of other CH(E)s which had recently undergone staffing alterations was finally agreed as follows:

Principal
2 deputy principals
10 teachers/instructors
Senior psychologist
Bursar
Assistant bursar
4 team leaders (scale 7)
12 senior residential social workers (scale 6)
21 residential social workers (scale 3/4)
3/4 supernumary RSWs for cover when other staff
   on training courses (scale 3)
2 clerical staff

Implications of the new staffing ratio

Apart from the obvious large increase in residential child care staff
in each house unit, we created, for the first time, no distinct division between male and female staff. We have already appointed two
female senior residential workers.

It was decided to dispense with the traditional roles of matron
and assistant matron. As the former was due to retire in February
1979 and the latter wished to apply for a senior residential post,
there was no internal conflict of disappearing roles. The new post
of bursar is not purely administrative, but takes in some of the
tasks of the former matron, as the assistant bursar does of the previous assistant matron.

We all felt that the role of senior psychologist was one that was
urgently needed at Ardale, to help implement and instigate the new
proposed philosophies. The traditional night supervisors disappeared
and become enmeshed with the role of residential workers. Although
all the night supervisors have been appointed as RSWs, it has been
agreed that, initially at least, their role will not drastically change
but, as they retire, the whole concept of general night supervision
may be looked at again.

There are a number of complicated matters regarding annual
leave. However, none of the staff in post have had any alteration
to their leave entitlement, and the newly appointed staff knew exactly what their leave entitlement was from the advertisements.

It was felt that with the reduction of boys by 40 per cent, that
we could not expect to have an increase in the teaching and instructional staff. At the time, this was accepted as being fair and logical,
but CH(E) teachers have recently had their working day reduced
and their annual leave increased by six weeks. Shortly, on the matter

of extraneous duty alone, we may have to have another review on the numbers of teachers and instructors at Ardale, as will most CH(E)s.

Structural alterations and modifications

From the very first discussion on a possible increase in staff, the whole matter of where they were going to be accommodated was considered. Similarly, in line with our new ideas on child care philosophy, certain modifications to the house units were felt necessary. As always, the question of finances kept cropping up. Luckily, the London Borough of Newham was able to obtain a large loan from the DHSS which had been originally allotted to another London borough who were unable to take up the offer for various reasons.

Our own school building department was able to carry out many minor modifications to the boys' house units. In two of them a large room had tended to become a junk room. It was designed in the approved school days as a boot room but was never used until we structurally altered it. In the two older houses, the addition or alteration of windows made many previously unused storerooms useful parts of the houses. The painting and decorating department got to work too and generally improved the standard of decor. Money was made available for some new carpets, curtains and furniture. The bedrooms, designed for a maximum of twenty-five boys were also modified so that many more could become single and double rooms instead of four-bedded rooms.

It was agreed to convert part of the school block complex into a central office area for senior and administration staff. This left a number of buildings available to be converted into extra staff accommodation.

It may be that we may eventually think of constructing a fifth house unit and the idea of some form of secure unit has not been completely ruled out.

Defining Ardale's new typologies

Apart from a very small number of CH(E)s, the policy of child care in many has drastically very little changed from the old approved school days. The same sort of boys, coming from the same sort of environment, with the same sort of problems and having committed the same sort of offences were being admitted into the CH(E) system of the 1970s. Ardale had been no exception to this. Bearing in mind

161

the theory that jacks of all trades are usually masters of none, Ardale began to take a very close look at just what type of delinquent child it could best help. The old idea that every type of boy with any sort of emotional, psychological or criminal problem could be helped under one roof was closely examined and eventually rejected.

It appeared obvious that the findings of the 'hard-core' experiment indicated that Ardale could possibly help a certain percentage of boys who would normally have been placed in some form of secure accommodation, although all were aware that, for many, treatment in security would be the only real answer. It is still possible that Ardale will, in the next few years, have a fifth, possibly secure house unit, specially built.

It was also felt that boys who showed disturbance through maladjustment and emotional insecurity could be helped at Ardale. Similarly, the more integrated neurotic delinquent boy (see p. 164) was also thought a likely candidate to be helped at Ardale.

The 'hard-core' experiment had taught a number of facts of the validity of a proper admissions procedure and it was eventually decided to turn the last of the four house units into a reception unit where boys would remain for the first few weeks of their stay in Ardale. When the new scheme had been in operation for some time, the ethos of the admissions house was looked at again. Although a certain section of this house still remains for admissions, the house has been combined with a group of what we term the more socialised delinquent (see p. 167).

The next few pages describe in greater detail the individual typologies of each of the present four house units. Early results tend to indicate that Ardale is on the right lines, but all concerned know that self complacency leads to stagnation of ideas. Ardale hopes to be flexible and on-going, and will certainly revise its policies as specific needs change.

Nansen House—the reception and admissions unit

In the past, many admissions to CH(E)s, Ardale included, have been on a random and fairly haphazard basis. This does not imply that there has been a lack of genuine care, but often there has not been a clear cut and distinct admissions policy. From an evaluation of the needs of delinquent boys, and our earlier experiences in admitting 'hard-core' boys we decided to create a house unit specifically to rectify that situation.

As explained earlier, all boys entering Ardale have had a full or paper assessment at one of the RACs, and the main aim of this section of Nansen House is not merely a perpetuation of this. The main aim of the admissions house is to hold and enable the boys to eventually fit into the typologies of one of the other four groups. This cannot be achieved without some period of specific assessment in relation to the known typologies of the other units. Obviously, prior to admission, a decision has already been made as to each boy's suitability to fit into one of the four units. If it is felt that none of these units has anything to offer to a boy, then he is not admitted.

The ethos of the admissions unit is, as far as possible, one of totally accepting a boy into the house, which is structured in an unobstrusive way. Lywood's term of 'stern love' probably sums up the regime better than any other. The total acceptance is one of firmness which enables a boy, on his first impression of Ardale, to realise that there are boundaries—boundaries to his own behaviour; boundaries to sub-unit behaviour; boundaries to the total community of Ardale behaviour; and, in turn, boundaries to society's behaviour.

The subsequent aims and tasks of the admissions unit team consist in the preparation of a 'Needs Assessment', based on each boy's individual needs, and the preparation of a twenty-four hour management programme. Such things as a boy's peculiarities with regard to waking, eating, relationships, his ability to relate to social workers, residential workers and educational staff, all have implications for further training within Ardale.

The role of the staff is of prime importance in this initial stage of a boy's stay at Ardale. Prior to his actual admission, each boy visits Ardale with his social worker and, whenever possible parents. He meets the staff with whom he will initially have considerable contact. These staff explain in simple terms such matters as suggested frequency of home leave or any specific query the boy may have. The staff present a welcoming approach while, at the same time, making it clear that the initial visit is not to decide whether or not the boy wishes to be admitted to Ardale, but whether Ardale feels it can help him and is willing to accept him.

Prior to arranging an informal visit, the system of deciding whether or not to consider a boy is now done on a team basis. The papers are sent to the principal who makes his initial comments on a special occurrence sheet attached to the case papers. If it is felt that we cannot help the boy, a special meeting is held to clearly elucidate our reasons. If we are all in agreement, the RAC is notified accordingly, stating our reasons quite clearly. If it is felt that we may be able to help a boy, the papers are passed to the two deputies, the team leader of the reception house and the team leader of the house it is felt the boy's needs indicate he will eventually move to. All comments are given in writing and, within forty-eight hours of receiving the papers, we contact the social worker and the RAC arranging a date for an initial visit.

In normal circumstances, boys remain in the admission house until their first case review—anything between three and six weeks after arrival. The date of his review is always decided on the day a boy is admitted so that he knows right from the start the likely date when he will transfer to his permanent house unit. We had learned from our mistakes with our earlier system of admissions in which boys formed such an attachment that they did not want to leave. All boys and all staff know that no boy stays in Nansen House much longer than a maximum of two months, and often considerably less, unless he has been deemed to become part of the permanent house group which lives side by side, and usually assists the new boys to Ardale. Any particularly strong relationships formed between boys and staff are not broken merely because a boy moves from the reception house to one of the other three. There is quite a considerable amount of cross communication between the four houses, and boys who are transferred from Nansen are not suddenly forbidden to re-enter it as though it never existed.

Nelson House—the unit for the integrated neurotic delinquent

One dictionary definition of 'integrated' states: 'a personality developed by the conscious attempt to weld into a harmonious whole its diverse aspects and abilities'. It is foolish to assume that any boy entering a CH(E) is a fully developed personality. Boys entering Nelson House, after their stay in the reception house have many and considerable problems, although not necessarily so severe as those boys being admitted into Shackleton and Scott (as described later). It has never been our intention to use Nelson House to accommodate boys who can be placed in no specific category. Prior to the new development, Ardale was prepared to admit boys who, despite whatever reason they had been placed on care orders, displayed no obvious symptoms of requiring anything but a general programme of basic education, control and care. With the boys now being admitted to Nelson House, there is almost inevitably signs of lack of maturity, poor self-image, neurosis and emotional instability. The term integrated is used in its broadest possible sense, and often as a comparison to the non-integrated boys in Scott House.

One of the first problems usually met in this house unit is a positive difficulty in communication with adults. Nelson House attempts to create an atmosphere where communication is not only possible but desirable. There is a regime of friendliness between boys and staff, but there is never any doubt who is the adult. Staff, however, do not put themselves in such positions that a boy cannot communicate because of barriers created by formality or pomposity.

The boys need considerable support on the positive areas of ego-development. Staff are seen as reliable, parental type figures; people on to whom the boys can transfer their unresolved conflicts in regard to their parents. Although the staff expect and even seek the positive transferrence of parental emotional anxieties, they do so as mature and considerate adults, not as substitute parents.

Nelson House creates an atmosphere in which boys can make a positive use of aggressions and verbal aggression. The staff are aware that acting-out is frequently attributable to a breakdown in communication. The boys are provided with and encouraged to accept the opportunities of taking some responsibilities as individuals and as a group. Boys are helped to accept a system of logical reparation for their deeds and actions.

Many of the boys in this house unit initially try and present themselves as slightly superior types, sometimes even rather omnipotent. They need help, therefore, in modifying harsh super-egos. Obviously, far more individual assessment is needed of these boys, and their individual needs are considered in great detail. There is frequently strong evidence of maternal deprivation, and much of the treatment is based on the assumption that disturbance to a greater or lesser degree is often directly relative to the lack of preoccupation by a mother in the formative years.

It is the main aim of Nelson House to provide such open channels of communication that the boys can learn to understand, regulate and control many aspects of their behaviour. The role of the sensible mature female figure in this house is, by virtue of this alone, of paramount importance.

Scott House—the unit for the disturbed and maladjusted delinquent

Because of the highly individual nature of each boy's problems in Scott House, the staffing ratio is slightly higher and no two boys are admitted within a week of each other in order to enable a definite period of adjustment and settling in to take place. The senior psychologist and visiting consultant psychiatrist concentrate much of their time and efforts with the boys in this house.

Evidence of disturbance can be shown in many ways—wildly acting-out and exhibitionism, overt and positive aggression to peers or staff, withdrawal, etc. It is the aim of this house to attempt to isolate the causes of the disturbance and, wherever possible, treat them. A number of specific areas can be identified and subsequent tasks outlined. By doing so, we are able to imply the type of ethos and regime in the unit. For example, deeply disturbed boys need containment of the destructive areas of their personality. Many delinquent ideas and phantasies the boys may have can be anticipated and confronted in advance of positive delinquent action. This, of course, is also true of the boys in the other house units.

It is essential that a dependence on adults is established as quickly as possible. Many of the boys in CH(E)s will act out with staff they can trust in a completely different fashion to their peers or staff they merely come into contact with. Staff in Scott House have to accept that, in many cases, the boys they work the hardest with will let them down much more frequently than the other boys. Many of the boys are seeking to justify why a particular adult has so much time for them and look for reasons to be rejected so that they can once again tuck them into the safe category of 'all adults are the same—they all reject me'. This calls for great patience and considerable skills on the part of the staff in this house. Staff need to be able to channel delinquent excitement and there is a need for open methods of communication at all levels.

Many of the boys can, for want of a better description, be described in the somewhat emotive term of psychopath or potential psychopath. Many of them in their early years, especially the birth to eighteen months period, have been severely damaged by a lack of parental, particularly maternal, preoccupation. With this type of boy, a limited and controlled use of regression therapy may be used, although it is not possible for a boy to regress if he has never progressed.

The use of regression techniques must always be planned and reliable. The senior and more experienced members of Scott House monitor these very carefully. They are aware that to encourage and actively participate in a boy's regression needs experience and learned skills. Nothing is more damaging to a boy of this type than a member of staff who goes along with his regression, but has not the ability to use it as a positive tool. Under no circumstances do we consider complete regression, in the Freudian sense, to be within the purview of our skills. This can only be handled by a skilled psycho-analyst and then only in a clinical setting.

We also try to contain the non-functioning areas of ego in a boy's personality—for example panics. It is essential to relate one ego functioning area to another and we have found that this is often best achieved through communication. One of the most difficult types to get through to are those boys who present themselves in such a way that they seem to have a shield around their chaos until relationships are formed. This is the type of boy who causes no problems for the first few weeks in the house, and less experienced staff begin to wonder why he is not with the more integrated group. As, however, he begins to form relationships with the staff and the group, his behaviour appears to deteriorate. The skilled staff in the house know that this is the time the boy needs the most help adjusting the world of Ardale to his own private and previously very personal chaos.

Another problem which is hard to deal with is that of withdrawal. Complete or partial withdrawal from peers and staff needs considerable skill and patience to overcome. Despite the apparent lack of interest being shown by the boy, it is essential that channels of communication—one sided though they may be at first—are opened. It is easy, but of no value whatsoever to ignore this type of boy in the fond belief that he will join in with the group when he is ready.

Unlike the other three house units, there can be no one specific aim in Scott House, unless it be to offer as much individual help as possible to each boy in the areas where it is most needed. No two boys are alike or have the same problem: this is general with all CH(E) boys but perhaps even more noticeable in Scott House. The staff are chosen to be sympathetic, mature people who have vast degrees of patience, but who set definite individual boundaries. It is one of the staff's responsibilities to see that the particular problems of a specific boy do not cause serious problems, harm or further disturbance to the other boys. Communication techniques and group therapy are the most common tools used in this house for the seriously disturbed boy.

Nansen House—the unit for the socialised delinquent

Towards the end of 1979 as numbers increased and the other three houses began to reach their optimum number, the whole concept of reserving a fifteen-bedded unit exclusively for new boys on admission had to be seriously studied. It was obvious that a specific admissions unit could not continue to function if it was impossible to transfer the boys after their first case review to one of the other units.

A number of meetings and discussions took place and various ideas were mooted and rejected: one of these being a kind of pre-release unit in which boys returned to Nansen House for their final few weeks before leaving. Neither boys nor staff thought that to move a boy for a third time, especially a boy who may have been in a permanent house for up to two years, was a good idea. By the middle of August 1979, when we had admitted almost thirty boys into the new system, we were able to sit down and evaluate the specific needs of the few boys we had not been able to accept and those boys who could possibly have been placed in a different unit, had we the typology. There seemed to be a reasonably steady flow of 'hard-core', disturbed and neurotic delinquents, but we noticed that we were beginning to admit a number of boys who seemed more mature and, who while quite often, were heavily delinquent, were much more socialised in their relationships with peers and staff. In many respects they became a stabilising influence on some of their more acting-out peers. In a number of ways, their needs were quite similar to the integrated neurotic delinquent, although they were less overtly aggressive and unco-operative.

D. J. West states:

> Social delinquents were boys who had failed to internalize
> certain middle-class standards; they identified themselves with
> rebelious peer groups, and experienced little guilt about their
> transgressions. Social delinquents, more often than other
> groups, came from large families, had delinquent siblings, and
> had parents who were lacking in moral example or discipline.
> (D. J. West 1967)

A quick check through the family and social backgrounds of a number of the boys we had accepted indicated that what Dr West stated was, in fact, borne out. Eventually, we came to the conclusion that if we were going to continue a unit specifically for admissions, but at reduced numbers, the ideal type of boy to live side by side with newly admitted boys would be this type of delinquent. We thus created, in the early autumn of 1979, a fifth unit which we termed the unit for the socialised delinquent.

It was agreed that this should be for a maximum of twelve boys, which would leave us at least three places vacant for admission purposes, although we were aware that once our numbers reached sixty, we could possibly have up to five or six boys in the admissions process depending upon how many boys were due to shortly leave from the other house units and go to work.

The main aim of this unit was to help reduce delinquency by mature adult relationships and a steady increase in personal and general responsibility. Bearing in mind that many of the boys came from homes where there had been little guidance, it was felt that the role of the key worker was of prime importance and, in many respects, he or she could be regarded more as a friendly adviser rather than a specific counsellor.

Personal responsibility was given by making the group responsible for helping new boys in all the many problems they had to encounter when first arriving at a CH(E). When a new boy made his pre-admission visit, one of the socialised group was always present to introduce him to Ardale in conjunction with the new boy's key worker. Whenever possible, these two boys were reintroduced on the day of arrival and, in the most pleasant sense, acted as a big brother to the new boy for the first few days after admission.

To distinguish the socialised delinquent group from the admissions group, the house rules were closely scrutinised and altered to cater for the more adult needs of the permanent house group. They were allowed to stay up later, carry out extra tasks and earn more money, and were never spoken to harshly by staff in front of the new boys. Although this typology was created after the others, it is showing very good results already.

Shackleton House—the unit for the 'hard-core' delinquent

The description of this house has been left to the last as its creation is almost exclusively based on the findings of the Ardale experiment outlined in detail in this book. It has been argued that delinquency is untreatable. On the other hand, there is considerable evidence that there are many boys going through the CH(E) system who can only be referred to as 'hard-core' delinquents and perhaps—even at the age of fourteen or fifteen—professional criminals. There is a strong feeling that this group of recalcitrant, intractable and persistent young offenders can only be dealt with by incarceration. Some of the evidence and results shown in the 1974-76 experiment would indicate that this is not always necessarily so.

When proposing to create a house unit for this type of boy, we had to look carefully at our aims and proposed methods. The Ardale experiment had shown that, to a certain extent, delinquency is treatable if the specific root causes have been carefully analysed and the appropriate help offered. The main aim, therefore of Shackleton House is to locate and, if possible, treat the individual fundamental causes of delinquency.

There are many different reasons why youngsters commit crimes, but one must never rule out self-gratification, the pursuit of pleasure, greed, boredom, and the need to be seen as part of the peer group sub-culture. It is fair to state that a small number of boys, even in their early teens, have already decided that the advantages of a criminal career far exceeds the possible retributions of society, including incarceration. To a small percentage, the thought of a possible Borstal or prison sentence is no real deterrent.and could be regarded as an occupational hazard.

Taking all our previous research findings, we felt that we could best define 'hard-core' delinquency for the general benefit of all staff as:

1 Boys who have persistently absconded from or seriously

disrupted previous residential establishments and may have been excluded from such places.

2 Boys who behave in a seriously disruptive fashion and act-out aggressively.

3 Boys, who by virtue of their behaviour, are a source of danger to themselves or others.

4 Boys who continue to commit offences despite all forms of treatment.

There are a number of other variables, less well-known. Many of the 'hard-core' group have suffered from some form of paternal deprivation; many commit offences alone rather than in the group situation normally associated with delinquent teenagers. Many coloured boys are included in this group merely because society does not know in which other category to place them, and the natural resentment of such coloured boys makes them appear far worse than they really are.

In many cases, because of paternal deprivation for whatever reason, a number of the boys have been thrust into a position of male superiority in their households, which many of them have not been able to cope with. There has often been a sad lack of a loving, but controlling, male figure in their lives. In Shackleton House, boys enter an atmosphere where the staff—particularly the male staff—are seen to be caring, mature, but above all consistent people. Boys soon learn that the staff will talk to them, listen to them, but that they impose boundaries on behaviour not only within Ardale but during any period away from it.

Numerous methods are used to help the boys to realise that their delinquent acts are not necessarily in their own best interests. Staff avoid talking down to the boys in a moralising or condescending fashion. The boys have heard times without number from other sources, how bad they are. Individual counselling with a member of staff they have learned to trust and perhaps respect, and various forms of group therapy plays a much more positive role than negative criticism. Each boy has access to his key worker on a regular basis. This is usually, but not necessarily, a male member of staff from Shackleton House. He or she must at all times be a mature person, able to offer help, comfort and advice, but also able to say 'No' when the need arises. The formulation of good staff / boy relationships is of prime importance and is encouraged while the boy is still in the reception house.

As one of the main problems of the boys being admitted into Shackleton House is a behavioural one, a definite programme of behaviour modification, based on a realistic appraisal relevant to each boy's age and experience, is a fundamental part of the treatment plan. This can consist of a combination of the following: group pressures; stress situations and stress interviews; intensive counselling; rewards and privileges schemes.

The educational aspect of these boys also receives close attention as it is pointless to continue an educational programme similar to that almost invariably rejected prior to being admitted to Ardale. Diagnostic and prescriptive teaching is used and much of the teaching is by objectives. By various means, all education is streamlined towards vocational work so that a sense of achievement and pride of doing a fair day's work for a fair day's pay can be obtained. Unless some form of positive work habit can be formed, there is often no alternative, in the boys' eyes at least, to continuing a criminal career.

All staff have a consistent attitude and refuse to condone criminal or nefarious behaviour. Incidents such as bullying become focal points in group discussions. The boys are aware that rewards and privileges are affected just as much by their behaviour at home on leave as within Ardale.

There has to be very close liaison with each boy's social worker and they have to understand that it is possible that such pressures as behaviour modification techniques may cause some boys to initially abscond. Similarly it is essential for evaluating efforts to request that each social worker provides follow-up information when a boy has left.

Many of the boys will not be successful in the classical sense. There must be failures and nobody can promise to transform some of the most difficult boys in this country into first rate and respectable citizens.

The concept of control in the newly developed Ardale

Ardale's new policies revolve around the concepts of care, treatment, control and education. The first two have been discussed in relation to the tasks set for each house unit: the latter is described in the next section of this chapter. What then of control? Such emotive words as control, discipline, punishment, sanctions, etc. have very different connotations for each individual. Let us try to elucidate what is meant by the concept of control at Ardale.

We must, from the very beginning, look closely at the types of boy entering the CH(E) system, their specific needs in all aspects of life, and the expectations of society. Many of the boys have suffered from a lack of basic parental control in their formative years. Many of them have never had a parent willing or capable of saying 'No you

171

can't'. In many cases, this inability to understand that all personal desires cannot be immediately gratified has led, however remotely, to a CH(E) placement being sought. Conversely, a number of boys, quite often from first generation West Indian families, have had a strict upbringing. Child battering in this country appears to be on the increase. It should be stated that there are times when a good slap around the legs for a young child is often the very best form of therapy, but to use corporal punishment as the only means of control becomes meaningless. Corporal punishment is never used at Ardale.

Control at Ardale is mainly a matter of formulating the proper sort of relationships with mature adults. It is not a matter of punishment and rigid sanctions.

To maintain an atmosphere where boys and staff can live in peace together there must be a system and framework of common sense rules and regulations. This is so in any walk of life. Nobody would be happy if the bullying of weak boys was ignored or the lads could decide to stop up all night if they desired. No rule at Ardale is ever made without a sound and logical reason. For example, boys are allowed to use the village shop, but certainly not in the middle of the classroom day if they feel like missing maths.

The boys do have some say in the formulation of rules, particularly in their own house units. However, some of the rules come directly from the staff. We firmly believe in a semi-democratic situation where the boys have a considerable say in the running of their daily lives, but we never intend to let democracy turn into chaos.

The majority of the sanctions used are discussed in detail with individual social workers and frequently become part of the treatment plan. For example, a boy who is a continual nuisance to his parents on weekend leave may, in full agreement at a case review, have his treatment plan so modified that he goes home less frequently. Obviously, the reverse also happens and some boys go home more often because of their improved behaviour at home.

Self control and the observation of common sense rules and regulations is just as much a learning process as group therapy and classroom education. It is quite easy to have control without care but it is not possible to have genuine care without some form of sensible control.

The concept of education at Ardale

Although Ardale does not refer to itself as Ardale School very often, it is still a place of education. We sometimes tend to fall into the trap of putting residential care and treatment before education.

This is a very common trap. In the early 1970s, when most approved schools became CH(E)s, the concept of education frequently tended to get swamped under by the concepts of care and treatment. The very important role of the teacher and the trades instructor, both as educators and in a pastoral capacity, was often ignored. Many people tended to forget the very important 'E' after 'CH'.

Ardale was able to look back objectively at the approved school system from experience. We are now entering the days of nostalgia for the good old approved school days, but in the early days of CH(E)s the removal of the word school often meant the removal of the need for any type of formal or even informal education. This was a false premise.

Every day more and more psychologists, researchers, social workers and parents are returning to the more sensible outlook and accept that the concept of education is just as important as that of care, treatment or control. Wisely, Ardale never replaced its teachers and instructors with residential social workers nor closed its trade departments in spite of the various pressures to do so when trade or vocational training was definitely the 'out thing'.

During the Ardale Development Committee's initial research the concept of care took a predominant role. To a certain degree, the valuable contribution of the teaching and instructional staff to the new concept of Ardale was put on one side. However, once the residential staffing ratios were decided, the whole concept of education at Ardale was studied and the educational staff invited to fully participate and contribute their ideas. Various meetings were held, and the following points were closely looked at:

1 The obvious different methods needed now that the high IQ criteria was not an essential prerequisite of admission into Ardale.
2 The role of the teacher—in an educational capacity—in a non-classroom situation. Was there a need for certain boys to follow some form of educational course within the safety of their own house units?
3 Could there be an improvement in the contributions made by teachers in their pastoral role?
4 Was there a place for female teachers in what had always been a male orientated domain?
5 The cessation of specialisation by some of the academic teachers.
6 The role of examinations with the small group still capable and desirous of sitting GCE and CSE.
7 The use of audio-visual techniques in both an education and a

counselling capacity.

8 The continuing use and possible expansion of vocational training as an important element in preparing boys for the future.

These were but a few of the points discussed. The fund of good will and genuine interest amongst the teachers and the instructors became obvious to everybody. Many felt that their valuable contributions had gone unnoticed in the past.

Ardale now has a teaching situation where some of the teachers are classroom based in a non-formal situation, some still teach by traditional methods, and one teacher is mainly house based with a group of new boys. We have turned one of the rooms in Nansen House into a learning centre. It was decided that to do away with all forms of traditional teaching would be wrong and foolish. Ardale is still a registered examination centre and those boys capable of taking external examinations need formal lessons if they are to succeed. House staff are encouraged to participate in classroom activities. The old notion that only teachers can teach has been widened in an acceptance that education is total and not just what a boy learns by sitting behind a desk in a formal classroom.

Vocational training, despite the earlier problems already mentioned, has always had a considerable role to play. The trade instructors are motivated to pass on their knowledge and skills to the boys in their groups. Luckily Ardale has well equipped workshops and many buildings the boys can practice joinery, painting, and building subjects on. Ardale has full instructional courses in: building, plastering and brickwork; carpentry and joinery; motor mechanics; engineering and welding and painting and decorating. The trades taught have been so chosen to coincide with many employment prospects in the areas the boys live in. The follow-up of types of jobs the school leavers have obtained has been a significant factor in deciding just which vocational opportunities should be available at Ardale. Quite often visitors and social workers ask why we do not give basic instruction in such subjects as cooking and horticulture. Apart from not having the staff nor the facilities for the former, it would seem ludicrous to teach horticulture to the boys when most of them come from the more industrialised areas of London and would have little chance to seek any form of employment in this sphere.

The deputy principal (education) is delegated considerable responsibility for the educational aspect of every boy. He and his two senior teachers spend a great deal of time with each new boy, drawing up a timetable which is an integral part of the general treatment programme. There is still a need for most boys to have a basic grounding in maths and English, and these have been retained as the only two compulsory subjects. Each boy is given the opportunity to try out the various trade training departments before making a final decision as to which one or two he wishes to follow with a possible view to making one of them his career when he leaves Ardale. Regular meetings between individual boys and the senior teaching staff allows for each educational plan to be on-going and gives boys the opportunity, for genuine reasons, to alter their course of study.

In a boy's final few months, usually following his final case review, he is encouraged to join the leavers group where he may go on a three week unpaid work experience project, and where most of his education is geared towards life outside Ardale—how to fill in a tax form or a football coupon, how to cook a simple meal, or mend a fuse or replace a tap washer, etc. Education at Ardale is just as important as care, treatment and control.

14 Conclusions and recommendations

The vacillating public—'care' or 'control'

It has long been a practice of mine to cut out from any newpaper
or magazine, articles which may have some relevance to the work
we are trying to do at Ardale. Before giving any further views, it
may be of some interest to quote from a few of these in order to
show some of the contrasting views on what this country could or
should do to the young delinquent.

> Today's ethics are that the child should have no responsibility
> with no demands made on him for tasks or other people. A
> vicious circle is fed by those who think that a child's boredom
> can be satisfied by 'more' leisure facilities, more entertainment.
> The 1969 Children and Young Persons Act is based on the idea
> that delinquency does not exist in its own right—it is merely a
> symptom of deprivation ... It's all a joke really; the tiny fines,
> conditional discharges, supervision orders, care at home are all
> seen as ways of 'getting off'. The delinquent may have been
> told many times he will be put away next time. Can you blame
> him for thinking it will never happen? (*Daily Mail*, 29 November
> 1978)

> A Chief Constable gave warning yesterday that repressing
> freedoms would not halt the rising crime rate. He said the key
> rested with teachers. The belief that repression was the only
> way to keep the peace would grow unless they helped to
> pioneer a new age of authority based on trust and understand-
> ing. (*Daily Telegraph*, 7 September 1978)

> Violence on a tremendous scale has erupted at London's largest
> assessment centre of disturbed juvenile offenders, social workers
> on the staff said yesterday. (*Daily Telegraph*, 25 August 1978)

> Britain's top policeman, Scotland Yard Commissioner Sir David
> McNee, last night demanded that young offenders should be
> punished and *not* treated as welfare cases by the country's
> courts. Sir David declared: Crime is anti-social and young
> offenders must be made aware of society's general disapproval.
> The failure to spell this out—in unequivocal fashion—has almost
> certainly contributed to the growth in crime. (*Sunday Express*,
> 9 July, 1978)

England is gradually emerging from the age of the institutions, when it was felt that the best form of care for persons in need of help or for people exhibiting deviant behaviour could generally be provided in large institutions run by experts. There is now considerable agreement that most people are best helped by providing services which will enable them to continue living in their own homes in their own lifestyle. (*Community Care*, 5 July 1978)

The number of indictable offences in England and Wales rose by 15 per cent last year to 2.64 million. A rise of 11 per cent to 195,000 was recorded in the number of persons aged between 10 and 17 found guilty or cautioned for indictable offences. (*Daily Telegraph*, 27 July 1978)

Remarkably little violence in community homes with education has been found by the researchers from Dartington Social Research Unit at Dartington Hall, Devon. It seemed possible to draw up a list of factors for identifying an institution which was likely to be violent. These included low staff morale, a high running away rate, and a low ratio of qualified staff. (*Community Care*, 20 September 1978)

Personally, I am very excited by the search for alternatives to institutional care which will hopefully be more appropriate to the needs and spirit of the present time. (*Community Home Schools Gazette*, December 1978)

A call to bring back approved schools for treatment of young offenders was made by Dr Rhodes Boyson, the Conservative education spokesman yesterday. Dr Boyson said: 'There is increasing evidence on all sides that the permissive society does not work'. (*Daily Telegraph*, 18 August 1978)

The startling conclusion (of a 1977 DHSS survey) is that in a large proportion of the cases, committal to care for delinquency is being used as a first or early response, not as a last resort. (*Social Services*, 2 May 1978)

Criminals choose their way of life and are not driven to it by circumstances. This is a claim which has split the criminology world like a cleaver. On one side are the hard men, policemen and prison warders, who applaud the rediscovery of truths they have long known; on the other, academics and social workers who mutter about a betrayal of scientific method and liberal values. (*Observer*, 4 June 1978)

Lord Justice Lawton yesterday appealed for a return to tougher discipline, and condemned the soft theories of well meaning but misguided sociologists, which he blamed as one of the causes of rising juvenile delinquency. (*Daily Telegraph*, 2 September 1978)

A school's ex-pupils wanted to give their teachers a lesson. So they bombarded them with obscene phone calls. They kept up the onslaught for four months—because they felt that the teachers had been too strict—two elderly women teachers, one of whom was a spinster ... Both boys were given supervision orders for two years and ordered to pay costs of £4.00 each. (*Sunday Mirror*, 18 February 1979)

I think that it would be rather pointless to make too many comments about the diversity of views when it comes to methods of dealing with today's delinquent youth. On one hand we have the 'lock 'em up and flog 'em' brigade, while at the other extreme we have the 'give them love and care and they will naturally get better' group. Neither is right, but neither is completely wrong. One has to look for the positive points from both extreme views.

The biggest problem when dealing with delinquents is that everybody thinks he is an expert. How often have residential workers heard a view being prefaced with: 'I've brought up two lads of my own and ...'? Many professions have their mystic rites and secrets; the medical profession being just one. However, everybody seems to be an amateur sociologist when delinquency is being discussed. There are experts in dealing with delinquency: people who have spent many years of their lives living with the problem, trying to do something about it, and CH(E) staff are amongst the largest body of experts in the practical aspects of dealing with delinquency in this country.

Was the Ardale 'hard-core' experiment a success?

By our definition of success both within Ardale and when boys had left, the answer must be 'yes'. Success, like any similar criterion must be relative, and ours was relative to the national statistics. The boys did no worse than the majority of boys leaving CH(E)s and in many respects better. To take a boy so steeped in delinquency and behavioural problems before entering Ardale and then expect every one of them to become model citizens is asking a bit too much. There is no easy answer but it must be accepted that no matter what forms of treatment or punishment are going to be used, the problem of juvenile crime will remain with us. Society has been asking what to do with teenage criminals since the days it ceased to hang and transport them. It will be asking the same question for many years to come.

The Ardale experiment is probably just one of many being attempted in various residential establishments. What Ardale set out to do has been done with some modicum of success. Without any form of secure provision and with a low staffing ratio Ardale managed to help some highly delinquent boys. The problems were enormous and knowing what we do now, it was probably slightly foolish to tackle the problem on such a shoe-string budget with such a skeleton staff.

As the school managers decided that the experiment should cease after two years because of the internal problems and the decrease in staff morale, it was perhaps a failure in this respect. As it helped to make everybody aware of the problems of too few staff having to deal with so many difficult boys, with the consequent re-development programme, it could be judged a success. Perhaps the best criteria of success will never be really known: how many of the 'hard-core' group will have children who grow up into 'hard-core' delinquents themselves? We may have done very little to help this generation, but only time itself will tell if we have been able to sufficiently guide them to help the next generation.

Implications for the future

Whatever methods we use now or in the future, juvenile delinquency will remain and will almost inevitably increase. Many academics, criminologists, sociologists, politicians, and psychologists have expounded what is needed to be done. I am often asked to forecast future trends in child related crime. This is not too difficult. What is difficult is to judge what can be done to help, treat or punish these type of young offenders. Too many people relate change with progress. The 1969 Act had many good and many weak points, but then again, so did the approved school system. One can sympathise with the police, but one must also have feelings for children who have been totally ignored by their parents and drift into crime through boredom or a desire to be part of a group. We can all feel sorry for a youngster leaving school with high aspirations who cannot find employment, but must we throw the blame on the 'blackies coming into this country', because a West Indian school leaver has to try that extra bit harder to get a job and is successful? We are all aware of the many problems of violence and plain insubordination teachers have to face in our state schools, but how much are we to blame with some of our trendy ideas? Who can have anything but deep concern that some old people are too terrified to leave their houses at night for fear of getting mugged, but what of the children who are battered day in and day out in their own homes?

We are a country of paradoxes. Cane them today and love them tomorrow. In the meantime, we have two forms of dealing with delinquency—residential and non-residential methods. Let us look at what implications this research has thrown up about either of these.

Community Homes

Excluding CH(E)s for a moment, we must remember that a community home can mean anything or nothing. The 1969 Act decided that all residential establishments for children would henceforth be known by the collective title of community home. How naive to think that by a mere change in nomenclature, all specialisation would be thrown out of the window. Ex-approved schools were the first to complain so the convenient 'E' was added to 'CH'.

There are too many and too few community homes. The mushroom growth of establishments that now call themselves observation and assessment centres is fantastic. The question one must ask is what are they observing the children for and when they have assessed them, are there the number of beds available in those community homes that do not specialise? There is a positive need to have emergency establishments that can quickly take in children at any time of the day or night—children who are being battered by their parents or whose family have been involved in a road accident. There are many community homes that should cease assessing children for other community homes, but get on with the business of helping those children who have to be taken into care.

Social work specialisation

Next to treatment and therapeutic, the most well worn word is generic. 'We're alright now we've gone generic'. It sounds like some contagious disease. In the approved school days there were child care officers. Some were good, some fair, and some pretty hopeless, but they all had one thing in common; they were not trying to be jacks of all trades and, by implication, masters of none. Their specific social work role was to deal with children. Not for them the problems of the aged or the mentally ill. However, the in-thing in the early 1970s was to go generic. All social workers are now supposed to be experts on all forms of social ills. Let us get back to sanity. We need specialists in the social services just as much as in the medical profession. After all, not many of us would be too happy about having open heart surgery performed by a gynaecologist or a brain tumour removed by an ear, nose and throat specialist. Why then should child care not be once again returned to specialists?

180

The future of the CH(E) system

It is now over ten years since the 1969 Act, so it should not be long before we have another one. It is perhaps worth thinking about that not one single Children and Young Persons Act this century has been fully implemented. The 1933 Act created approved schools: the 1969 Act created CH(E)s, what will the next act create? Remember that the buildings, the facilities, the staff and the fund of experience remains no matter what the actual philosophy changes are. Before we had approved schools we had reformatories and before that we had workhouses. Remember too we have had delinquent children in the past, we have them today, and we are still going to have them in the future.

What then are we going to do with them? Is it possible to help them all in the community by fostering, intermediate treatment, or non-penal sentences? Should we lock them all away in heavy security? How about the short sharp treatment being advocated as though it were something new?

However, what is likely to happen to teenage delinquents for the next decade or so at least is that some will be dealt with in the community and some will go into residential establishments. We may not talk of intermediate treatment or CH(E)s but in many cases the treatment will be a rose by any other name. There just aren't sufficient alternatives that work or even appear likely to work to dispense with all residential training and treatment for all delinquent youth. The prisons and Borstals are too full now, a detention centre is usually of only six actual weeks length, and a residential placement is often the most suitable form of resource not only to help a delinquent child come to terms with himself, but to give society a brief respite from him and his nefarious activities.

What do our CH(E)s of the future need?

Earlier, when talking of field social workers, I strongly advocated a return to specialisation. A CH(E) by its very nature is a specialist form of residential establishment. In the main it has much better qualified, experienced and paid members of staff than any other residential facility for children, delinquent or not. However, over the last decade, many have been taken in by the so called therapeutic approach and, if you like, gone generic. At one time, most senior boys' approved schools had thriving trade departments but so many have been swept away that I could say that by keeping and enlarging our vocational training programme, one of Ardale's specialisations could be useful trade training.

181

There are too many CH(E)s all striving to do the same thing and competing with each other. Because of this and the ever rising cost of a CH(E) placement, social workers are ringing around not to ask what have you got to offer for my boy if he comes to you, but what are your costs? If each regional planning authority had a host of specialist CH(E)s, the right boy may go to the right place.

Despite the extremely high cost of youth treatment centres, they seem to be having some success. Is is not now time that the CH(E) system adapted some of its establishments along these lines? There is talk of a new secure care order. Where are the children going to go if there are no secure places for them? There is probably a need to create one or two secure CH(E)s up and down the country. These need to be well planned and well staffed. The Ardale experiment showed that in many respects some 'hard-core' delinquents could be helped, but many more could be helped in a more secure environment provided that care was always as important as control.

Many CH(E)s are suffering from the approved school philosophy of building them in the country away from areas of population. Most of us agree that this was a wrong idea and that the 1969 Act was right in regarding a reasonable proximity from the home area to be of considerable importance. After all, if a boy is going to abscond, he will do so if he lives 400 or forty miles away. Provided there are good rail, bus or road links close by and the majority of the boys can be home three or four hours after leaving a CH(E), lines of communication are open. It may be necessary to review some of the more inaccessible CH(E)s and perhaps make alternative uses of them. Geographical location of a CH(E) is of very considerable importance. Some CH(E)s may have to close or be adapted for other purposes purely because of their inaccessibility. Even if a few secure CH(E)s are built, they also must be within a few hours travel of the homes of the boys who will occupy them.

The most obvious finding of this research and one which many other groups and bodies are now aware of is that the staffing ratio of the approved schools is just not good enough for the level of care required at most CH(E)s. The main reason the experiment was terminated after just two years was that Ardale did not have sufficient staff. By having to take staff from other duties, it caused problems which eventually led to a drop in staff morale. It is only now, with a considerably increased staff, that we are once again able to help the 'hard-core' delinquent. This has quite serious fiscal implications, especially for those CH(E)s that are run by voluntary organisations and who are existing on a shoe-string budget. As staff numerically increase in CH(E)s, so the costs too must inevitably rise. However, there are no 'ifs and buts' about this point. A CH(E) can only be fully efficient if it has sufficient staff to do more than merely contain children. This, perhaps more than anything, was one of the failings of the approved school system, and was so clearly shown by the 'hard-core' experiment.

As staff in CH(E)s increase, their conditions of service, salaries and promotion prospects must also be closely examined. There are almost as many anomalies in the system as there are in the ordinary community home system. One fact is obvious: staff in CH(E)s are the highest paid of any residential staff. In comparison with many residential workers in other community homes this is true, but when compared to the national statistics, they are very much under paid. The average residential worker is a very poorly paid person indeed.

Then we have the other anomaly of a CH(E). Because we have education on the premises we not only have residential workers on the staff, but qualified and certificated teachers and trade instructors. Here are two more levels of salary. The teachers are paid on a special rate of the Burnham Scale, which includes the approved school allowance. Many of the senior staff are qualified teachers and are paid on yet another rate of the Burnham Scale. The instructors may be partly or substantially qualified, each with its individual scales of pay. The teaching staff have now obtained parity with teachers in special schools with an increase in annual leave from eight to fourteen weeks. This is excellent as far as recruitment is concerned, but it makes any blending of teaching and residential staff in a CH(E) just that extra bit more difficult.

All these different salary scales and conditions of service would not be too bad if they were standard in CH(E)s up and down the country, but even this is not so. As many of them still work on the approved school scales, the few which have developed and changed usually have different and, in most cases, better, conditions of service. So we may get the senior member of staff running a house unit in CH(E) One earning as much as £700 a year less than one doing a similar job in CH(E) Two. Even titles and nomenclature are no longer standard. We still have principals or headmasters or officers in charge of CH(E)s; we have wardens or team leaders; housemasters or residential social workers. Naturally, when a CH(E) makes a radical change in staffing, everybody insists on protected salaries and conditions of service for those staff already in post who may not get one of the newly created promotion posts. However, at Ardale we hope that this anomaly will iron itself out over a period of the next few years as staff seek promotion and move to pastures new. What we need soon is a national look at salaries and conditions of service for staff in all CH(E)s. This was simple when we all came under central government, but it is much more difficult now. Perhaps

CH(E)s should return to a central government umbrella.

Still on the subject of residential staff, the experiment taught me that those staff who had received formal training were able, in the main, to cope much better than those who had not yet done so. Generally, the teachers were able to cope much better than the majority of the untrained residential staff, but the mainstays of the experiment were those staff who had taken and successfully completed a one or two year training course leading to the Certificate in Residential Child Care. Built into our new system are three or four full time supernumary residential workers to allow three or four staff per annum to attend full or part time courses, such as the Certificate in Social Services. At the present moment, there are two staff on a full time Certificate in Child Care Course, one on a CSS course, and one on a CQSW course. Two other staff hope to be considered shortly for the CSS course. This latter form of training is fairly new and was regarded with a certain degree of scepticism at first by many people. However, it is tailored to each student's particular needs. The only worry is that it takes up so much of a student's time, apart from the two days at college, that it is about time it ceased to be called a part time course. Residential workers being seconded to CQSW (Certificate of Qualification in Social Work) are now on the increase. According to a report in *Social Work Today*, 13 February, 1979, the number of residential workers attending a two year course in CQSW has increased from 63 in 1975 to 155 in 1978. Still only a dismal proportion when compared to the number of field social workers who are seconded, but definitely a step in the right direction. If CH(E)s are going to be able to offer a positive service, there must be recruitment of a much better qualified member of staff, and an increasing opportunity for junior staff to attend courses so that they can be helped to do their job better and to seek promotion within the service.

Returning for a moment to the various methods children get to CH(E)s and the selection criteria of such establishments, it has been stated that if CH(E)s all had policies outlining which particular type of child they could best help, the problems of ensuring that each child went to the right CH(E) would be considerably reduced. There is talk of the possible creation of a secure care order but nobody really knows what that means. If it means that children placed on such orders will have to go to a CH(E) with a secure unit or a youth treatment centre, then the sheer lack of places will make this almost impossible to implement. It could even mean a spate of badly planned and not very secure units being hastily thrown up at most existing CH(E)s.

A few selected CH(E)s up and down the country probably need

to go secure, but there must be very careful planning, quite a considerable amount of money poured into them, and they must have a high staff ratio with definite policies for selection and treatment. Even a secure CH(E) would not survive if it was expected to take every type of child thrown at it. There would need to be different types of secure CH(E)s with different qualified staff running them. The most obvious and logical solution is to have some form of care order which differentiates between the present one where the social services department can decide what they intend to do with a child and sometimes ignore any recommendations by magistrates. Because magistrates are seeing the same child appear before them so frequently, they are having to resort to detention centre orders in the knowledge that, for six weeks at least, the general public will have a short respite from them. Magistrates need the power to place a child on a care order in the sure knowledge that the child will receive residential training and treatment. What I am advocating is almost a return to the approved school order. Whether this is called a secure order, a CH(E) order or what you will, the fact is that many children are just not receiving residential help because of the present legal system. It is not unlikely that the system will sometimes be abused and that sometimes a child will be ordered into residence who could be best helped without it, but there has been such a gigantic upsurge in juvenile crime since children learned—and they learned quickly—that if they were caught they had a very strong chance of getting away with it on a care order. The present system of care orders is weak and ineffective: it must change and it needs to change very soon.

If a new form of care order is created and put into implementation, it would have numerous implications for CH(E)s. Once again a system of specialist CH(E)s could be organised instead of the present method whereby most of them admit some children they are not really equipped to positively assist. There could still be opportunities for children on ordinary care orders to be helped in most CH(E)s. I am not advocating the system, so loved by the approved schools, of each having one particular specialisation, such as Ardale's grammar school image. The only result of this would be that children would have to be sent further and further away from home for help. What is needed is for the Regional Planning Committees to regularly meet with the senior staff of all CH(E)s in their region and with the directors of social service departments who administer the CH(E)s and to form a pool of treatment resources. At the moment, and excluding the admissions house, Ardale feels that it can cope with four specific problems—'hard-core' delinquents, maladjusted and disturbed delinquents, integrated neurotic delinquents, and socialized delinquents. If all the CH(E)s had this form of internal specialization, and a pooling system of knowledge was shared between regional planning officers, DHSS, social service departments, and heads of CH(E)s, there would be a much better chance of putting the right child in the right CH(E) where the most positive help could be offered.

Other implications for the future

Early in 1979, Ardale employed its first senior coloured member of staff: a West Indian gentleman with considerable residential experience. He has the very responsible position of being in charge of the house unit for maladjusted and disturbed boys. This book has indicated that the considerable increase in the coloured population in CH(E)s calls for specialist knowledge never really obtainable from somebody who has not experienced the many very real problems of being born or coming to this country with a dark coloured skin. It is not that CH(E)s have gone out of their way to show racial discrimination; just the reverse in fact. The main problem is that there are so few West Indian or Asian residential social workers.

Throughout the CH(E) service there is very close communication between staff at all levels, particularly senior staff. In a way, we are almost like a closed shop. This does not mean that staff from other disciplines cannot get into the work at a senior level, but in the main there is a definite promotion structure and well over 80 per cent of present heads have come up the ladder within educational residential work. They know the problems of their junior staff as they have experienced the same problems themselves. Even more important, there is a bond of trust between them. Heads communicate regularly and meet as often as possible. In the London area the Association of Heads of South Eastern CH(E)s is a very strong body and, because of our fund of knowledge, we are listened to and consulted at all levels.

Although we heads communicate with each other on many matters we are very weak on selling ourselves to the general public and the mass media. We, who have so much say in residential child care practices in this country, need to publicise much more often what we do and to point out to the mass media of our successes as well as the usually reported failures. Many articles are written by us in trade journals but then we are merely preaching to the converted. The editorial of the *Community Home Schools Gazette* (August 1979) puts this fact very clearly:

> As a body of professionals we are abject amateurs when it comes to public relations. It is about time we adopted a

186

more strident approach to selling our product to the consumer. There is a need to examine the nature of the criticism being directed at our schools and to respond in an appropriate manner. I suspect that the CH(E)s which survive the coming onslaught will be those which can prove the validity of their existence.

The final word

By showing that it is possible to help the most difficult type of teenage delinquent in this country in a CH(E), I have gone out of my way to sell the CH(E) system to all who read this book. Some may agree with me, many will disagree, but my main hope is that it has made you all think. I have decided that the final word shall not be mine, but one of the original 'hard-core' boys who visited my wife and I earlier this year, almost four years after he left Ardale:

> My younger brother is in Borstal now. I only wish that he had been given the same chance as I was. When I left I never expected to want to come back and visit, but do you know, the year and a half I spent here was definitely the most important time in my life.

Bibliography and further reading list

Aichorn, A., *Wayward Youth*, Imago (1925)

Anderson, R., *Representation In The Juvenile Court*, Routledge & Kegan Paul (1978).

Andry, R., *Delinquency & Parental Pathology*, Methuen (1960).

Arden, N., *Child of a System*, Quartet Books (1977).

Ball, C., et al, *Education for a Change*, Penguin (1973).

Bayley, D., *Police & Society*, Sage Publications (1977).

Becker, W., *Parents Are Teachers*, Research Press (1971).

Beedell, C., *Residential Life With Children*, Routledge and Kegan Paul (1969).

Belson, W., *Juvenile Theft: The Causal Factors*, Harper and Row (1976).

Bion, W., *Experiences In Groups*, Tavistock Publications (1961).

Boss, P., *Social Policy & The Young Delinquent*, Routledge and Kegan Paul (1967).

Burt, C., *The Young Delinquent*, University of London Press (1925).

Butcher, H., *Human Intelligence*, Methuen (1968).

Carlebach, J., *Caring for Children in Trouble*, Routledge and Kegan Paul (1970).

Cawson, P. *Community Homes: A Study of Residential Staff*, HMSO (1978).

Chaffin, J. and Kroth, R., *Workshop on Behaviour Modification*, Hammond (1971).

Clarizo, H. and McCoy, J., *Behaviour Disorder in School Aged Children—Journal of Special Education*, (1970).

Clarke, R. and Martin, D., *Absconding from Approved Schools*, HMSO, (1971).

Clegg, A. et al, *Children in Distress*, Penguin (1968).

Cloward, R. and Ohlin, L., *Delinquency & Opportunity*, Glencoe Free Press (1955).

Cohen, A., *Delinquent Boys: the Culture of the Gang*, Glencoe Free Press, (1955).

Cohen, S., *Property Destruction: Motives and Meaning*, Architectural Press (1973).

Cornish, D. et al, *Residential Treatment and its Effects on Delinquency*, HMSO, (1975).

Cowell, C., *Diary Analysis — A Suggested Technique for the Study of Children's Activities and Interests*, OUP, (1937).

Croft, J., *Research in Criminal Justice*, HMSO, (1978).

Curtis Report on the Care of Children, HMSO (1946).

Dartington Social Research Unit, *A Comparative Study of 18 Boys' Approved Schools*, (unpublished) (1972).

DHSS Development Group, *Development of Secure Provision in Community Homes*, (1974).

Docker-Drysdale, B., *Therapy in Child Care*, Longman, (1968).

Dominian, J., *Marital Breakdown*, Penguin (1968).

Douglas, T., *Basic Groupwork*, Tavistock (1978).

Douglass-Savage, R., *Psychometric Assessment of the Individual Child*, Penguin (1968).

Downes, D., *The Delinquent Solution*, Routledge and Kegan Paul, (1966).

Du Cane, E., *The Punishment & Prevention of Crime*, (1885).

Dunlop, A., *The Approved School Experience*, HMSO, (1975).

Ericson, R., *Young Offenders & Their Social Work*, Saxon House, (1975).

Eysenck, H., *Dimensions of Personality*, Routledge and Kegan Paul, (1947).

Eysenck, H., *Crime and Personality*, Routledge and Kegan Paul, (1964).

Eysenck, H., *Race, Intelligence & Education*, Temple Smith, (1971).

Ferrero, G., *Criminal Man: According to the Classification of Lombroso*, (1911).

Finlay, F., *A Boy in Blue Jeans*, Robert Hale, (1969).

Fyvel, T., *The Insecure Offender*, Penguin, (1961).

Gelfrand, D., and Hartman, D., *Behaviour Therapy with Children - Psychology Bulletin No. 69*, (1968).

Gittins, J., *Approved School Boys*, HMSO, (1952).

Glass, D., *Social Mobility in Britain*, Routledge and Kegan Paul, (1954).

Glueck, S. et al, *Unravelling Juvenile Delinquency*, Harvard University Press, (1950).

Glueck, S. et al, *Physique & Delinquency*, Harper, (1956).

Gray, J., *The Psychology of Fear and Stress*, World University Library, (1971).

Grunsell, R., *Born to be Invisible*, Macmillan (1978).

Hart, T., *Safe as a Seesaw*, (1976).

Herbert, M., *Problems of Childhood*, Pan Books, (1975).

HMSO, *Care and Treatment in a Planned Environment*, (1972).

HMSO, *Community Homes. A Study of Residential Staff*, (1978).

Hull, C., *Principles of Behaviour*, Appleton, Century, Crofts, (1943).

Jones, A., *Counselling Adolsecents in Schools,* Kogan Press, (1977).
Jones, M., *The Therapeutic Community,* Basic Books, (1953).
Jahoda, M. (editor), *Attitudes,* Penguins, (1966).
Krasner, L. et al, *Research in Behaviour Modification,* Holt, Ronehart & Winston, (1968).
Laslett, R., *Educating Maladjusted Children,* Crosby, Lockward, Staples, (1977).
Lovell, K., *An Introduction to Human Development,* Macmillan, (1968).
Lywood, G., *A Successful Experiment in Education,* Heinemann, (1964).
Mason, P., and Hoghugi, M., *Details of Study from 'Community Care',* (1978).
Mayers, M., Unpublished Thesis *Leisure Activities in the Special School,* (1971).
Mayers, M., Unpublished Thesis *A Comparative Evaluation of Group Work & Sociometric Testing,* (1973).
Mayers, M., Unpublished Thesis, *A Critical Evaluation of Assessment Facilities,* (1973).
Marsh, P., *Aggro—the Illusion of Violence,* Dent & Sons, (1978).
Merlen, B., *The Division,* Pelican, (1967).
McCord, W. et al, *Psychopathy & Delinquency,* Grune and Stratton, (1959).
Miller, D., *Growth to Freedom,* Tavistock, (1964).
Miller, F. and Kvaraceus, *Delinquent Behaviour: Culture and the Individual,* OUP, (1959).
Millham, S. et al, Unpublished Research *A Comparative Study of 18 Boys' Approved Schools,* (1972).
Millham, S. et al, Unpublished Research *Research at Risley Hall,* (1974).
Millham, S. et al, *After Grace—Teeth,* Chaucer Pub., (1975).
Millham, S. et al, *Locking up Children,* Saxon House, (1978).
Morris, A. et al, *Juvenile Justice,* Heinemann, (1978).
Moos, R., *Correctional Institutions Environment Scale Manual,* John Wiley & Sons, (1973).
Moos, R., *Evaluating Correctional and Community Settings,* John Wiley & Sons, (1975).
National Children's Bureau, *Who Cares?,* (1977).
Nunnally, J., *Psychometric Methods,* McGraw Hill, (1967).
Packham, J., *The Child's Generation,* Blackwell, (1975).
Page, M. et al, (editors) *Who Cares?,* NCB, (1977).
Paley, J. et al, *Children: Handle with Care,* National Youth Bureau, (1974).
Pavlov, I., *Conditioned Reflexes,* OUP, (1927).

Pearson, G., *The Deviant Imagination*, Macmillan, (1975).
Pedley, F., (editor), *Education & Social Work*, Pergammon, (1977).
Personal Social Service Council, *A Future for Intermediate Treatment*, (1977).
Poteet, J., *Behaviour Modification*, University of London Press, (1973).
Priestley, P. et al, *Justice for Juveniles*, Routledge and Kegan Paul, (1977).
Raisbeck, B., *Law & the Social Worker*, Macmillan, (1977).
Rennie, Y., *The Search for Criminal Man*, Lexington, (1978).
Renvoize, J., *Web of Violence*, Routledge & Kegan Paul, (1978).
Richardson, K. et al, *Race, Culture & Intelligence*, Penguin, (1972).
Romig, D., *Justice for our Children*, Lexington, (1978).
Rose, G., *Schools for Young Offenders*, Tavistock, (1967).
Rose, M., *The East End of London*, Crescent Press, (1951).
Rutter, M., *Maternal Deprivation Reassessed*, Penguin, (1972).
Saynell, R., *Mary Carpenter of Bristol*, OUP, 1964).
Schonell, F., *Backwardness in the Basic Subjects*, Oliver and Boyd, (1942).
Schonell, F., *Scholastic Diagnostic & Attainment Testing*, Oliver and Boyd, (1960).
Scott, J., *Aggression*, Cambridge University Press, (1958).
Sheldon, W., *Varieties of Delinquent Youth*, Harper, (1949).
Skinner, B., *About Behaviourism*, Jonathan Cape, (1974).
Slater, S., *Approved School Boy*, William Kimber, (1967).
Smith, P., *Group Processes*, Penguin (1970).
Stott, D., *Studies of Troublesome Children*, Tavistock, (1966).
Terry, J., *A Guide to the Children's Act 1975*, Sweet and Maxwell, (1976).
Thrasher, F., *The Gang*, Chicago University Press, (1927).
Timms, N., *The Receiving End*, Routledge and Kegan Paul, (1973).
Tutt, N., *Care or Custody*, Darton Longman & Todd, (1974).
Vernon, P., *Intelligence & Attainment Tests*, University of London Press, (1960).
Vernon, P., *Personality Assessment*, Methuen (1969).
Walter, J., *Sent Away*, Saxon House, (1978).
Walton, H., (editor), *Small Group Psychotherapy*, Penguin, (1971).
West, D., *The Young Offender*, Penguin, (1967).
West, D., *Present Conduct & Future Delinquency*, Heinemann, (1969).
West, D., *Who Becomes Delinquent?*, Heinemann, (1974).
West, D. et al, *The Delinquent Way of Life*, Heinemann, (1977).
Westley, W., *Violence & the Police*, MIT Press, (1970).
Whitacker, B., *The Police*, Penguin, (1964).
Whitman, J., *Behaviour Modification in the Classroom*, Clinical Pyschology Publishing Co., (1971).

Willmott, P. et al, *Family & Class in a London Suburb,* Routledge and Kegan Paul, (1960).

Wills, K., *Spare the Child,* Penguin, (1971).

Wilson, H., *Delinquency & Child Neglect,* Allen & Unwin (1962).

Winnicott, C., *Child Care & Social Work,* Codicatoe (1964).

Yablonsky, L., *The Violent Gang,* Macmillan, (1962).

Plus numerous articles from newspapers, magazines, and Home Office Reports (each time acknowledged).

Glossary

These are terms used mainly by the boys but in common usage amongst most people who come into contact with delinquent boys in Great Britain.

Beak	Usually a magistrate, but can also refer to a Crown Court judge.
Bird	Usually refers to present girl friend: e.g. 'My bird', but can refer to any female.
Bouncer	A person (usually powerful male) appointed to keep order at a club, disco or public house.
Bovver	Delinquent excitement or fun, often—but not exclusively—involved with violence. 'We're going out for some bovver tonight'.
Con	A trick or a dodge usually used to avoid trouble or work. To con a member of staff usually denotes that member of staff is naive or young or inexperienced.
Conkers	A seasonal British game played with the fruit of the horse-chestnut tree.
Copper	A policeman.
Fuzz	A policeman—becoming more fashionable than the word copper.
Gear	Clothing, mode or style of dress
Getting picked up	Being arrested or apprehended by the police on suspicion of going to commit a crime.
Grassing	Informing to the police or person in authority about some criminal activity of a friend or colleague.
Having collar felt	To be arrested or apprehended by the police.
Nicking	Stealing—usually petty crime.
Old Bill	The police—not used in many areas of Great Britain outside the London area, where there it is the most popular euphemism for the police.
Old man (at home)	Father.
Old man (in CH(E))	The principal or headmaster.
Old woman/old lady	Mother.
On the dole	Unemployed.

Putting the boot in	To kick a victim or rival, usually when he or she is on the ground.
The law	The police. Common usage with delinquent boys but less popular than 'Old Bill' in London area.
The '69 Act	The Children and Young Persons Act 1969, which abolished approved school orders and created care orders. Usually referred to with some contempt by those delinquent children intelligent enough to know its general contents.
Sent to DC	Awarded a three or six month sentence to a detention centre by a juvenile or magistrate's court.
DC remission	In most cases, a three month DC sentence usually amounts to a mere six weeks unless something serious has happened. This is due to serious shortage of places and, to many delinquent children, makes a detention centre sentence something trivial.
Slag	A female who prostitutes herself, but not necessarily a 'professional'. Some boys refer to their mothers as 'old slags'.
Sus	Short for suspicion, and refers to the police apprehending a person on suspicion of going to commit a crime or as a suspicious person. Tends to be over-used with coloured youth in the London area who are often apprehended 'on sus' if more than two or three congregate together.

Name index

Aichorn, A., 147

Baden-Powell, R., 138
Barnardo, T., 1
Becker, W., 41
Belson, W., 5ff
Bion, W., 38
Bowlby, J., 134
Boyson, R., 177
Burt, C., 93

Callaghan, J., 2
Carpenter, M., 1
Chaffin, J., et al., 40
Clarke, R., et al., 11ff
Clarizo, H., et al., 121
Clegg, A., 4
Cloward, R., et al., 13
Cohen, A., 13
Cohen, S., 13
Cowell, C., 47

Dickens, C., 1, 134
DuCane, E., 1
Duke of Edinburgh, 138

Friend, P., 151

Gelfrand, B., et al., 40

Halpin, H., 7
Hoghugi, M., 10, 51
Hull, C., 40

Johnson, S., 102

Lawton, Lord Justice, 177
Lombroso, C., 3
Lywood, G., 163

Marsh, A., 16

Mason, P., 10
McCord, W., et al., 3
McNee, D., 176
Miller, F., et al., 14
Millham, S., et al., 102, 144
Moos, R., 63ff, 78ff

Pavlov, I., 40
Pidduck, C., 4ff
Poteet, J., 40

Rutter, M., 134

Saynell, R., 1
Schonell, F., 93ff
Shaftsbury, Lord, 1
Sheldon, W., 3
Skinner, B., 40

Thorndyke, E., 40
Tutt, N., 3ff, 142, 151

Watson, L., 40
West, D., 3ff
Whitman, J., et al., 40

Subject index

Abnormal offenders, 9ff

Absconding, 11ff, 17, 33, 28, 87, 102ff, 119, 123, 145, 182

Admission procedures, 26, 61ff, 117

Aggression, 12ff, 40, 102, 117, 165

Alcohol—misuse of, 126, 139

Alternatives to CH(E)s, 125, 141ff 177, 181

American research, 13, 76ff, 86

Approved schools, 2ff, 10ff, 21ff, 27, 39, 97ff, 102ff, 116, 148, 161, 176ff, 183

Assessment, 49, 51ff, 78, 162

Behaviour modification, 20, 37, 38ff, 76ff, 88, 144, 170

Boards of guardians, 1

Borstal, 2, 89, 101, 108, 134, 150, 169, 181, 187

Bullying, 88, 119, 170ff

Capital punishment, 1, 39, 178

Care and control, 3, 18, 20, 30, 110, 116, 154, 170ff, 176ff, 182

Case conferences/reviews, 50, 100, 164, 172, 175

CH(E)s—general, 10, 24, 39, 44, 76, 101, 108, 111, 113, 115, 121, 124, 125, 131, 135, 140ff, 148ff, 153, 161, 180, 181ff.

Childrens Act 1908, 1

Childrens Act 1933, 1ff

Childrens Branch—Home Office, 1

Children and Young Persons Act, 1969, 2, 9, 18, 21, 51, 141, 154, 176, 180, 181, 182

Co-education in CH(E)s, 148ff

Commission for Racial Equality, 23

Community Homes—general, 11, 51, 61, 180, 183

Community Homes Schools Gazette, 4, 27, 102, 155, 177, 186

Community Home Regulations, 86

Community Service Orders, 150

Community work, 92, 151ff

Community service volunteers, 21, 119, 142, 151ff

Comparison groups, 25ff, 27, 45, 53ff, 63ff, 80ff, 123ff

Corporal punishment, 42, 86, 172, 180

Counselling, 20, 35ff, 76, 83, 91, 168, 174

Courts—general, 2, 7, 28, 56, 122, 125ff, 185

Criminal Justice Act 1972, 150

Criminal statistics, 1, 5, 11, 17, 58, 103ff, 121, 123ff, 154, 177

Curtis Report, 34

Dartington Research Team, 102

Delinquency—general, 1, 3ff, 9ff, 16ff, 38, 113ff, 137, 154, 164ff

Detention centres, 8, 28, 123, 124, 134, 181, 185

DHSS, 2, 186

Drugs, 39, 58, 126, 139

Education in CH(E)s, 20, 32, 44ff, 54, 59, 92ff, 172ff

The Author

Michael Oscroft Mayers, known as Mike to his friends, was born in Nottingham in 1937, although most of his working life has been spent in the north of England. He served his National Service in the Royal Air Force and later continued this interest as Flight Lieutenant and commanding officer of an Air Training Corps squadron.

Initially trained as a teacher at St John's College, York (now the College of Ripon and York St John), he switched to residential education after less than two years teaching in a primary school. He has worked in special schools, approved schools, and CH(E)s as a teacher, a teacher/housemaster, a third-in-charge, a deputy headmaster and, since 1973, Principal of Ardale CH(E). One of his claims is that he is aware of many of the problems of his staff, having worked through them himself at some time or another.

Having always had an interest in research work and lecturing, he has obtained a number of extra qualifications to enable him to carry out his work better. Apart from his Teaching Certificate, he holds a diploma in special education, a certificate in theology, the advanced diploma in educational rehabilitation of young people, and he is a Fellow of the College of Preceptors.

During the interim period, when approved schools ceased to exist and CH(E)s were very much in their infancy, the previous headmaster of Ardale School retired. As Mike says, Newham, Ardale and himself inherited each other at the same time and, in the main, it has been a very happy relationship.

He has great confidence in the CH(E) system but is aware that there may have to be alterations in the general concept of residential child care over the next decade or so. He is not opposed to secure accommodation on a CH(E) campus provided it is used as an integrated treatment facility and not merely a junior lock up in the grounds of an open establishment. There is a great deal of work still to be done to help delinquent children, he says, but the main needs of a successful Principal are an ability to combine genuine care with basic control, education, firm aims and policies, an organisational and managerial ability, a tight grip on administration, an ability to delegate, confidence, a sense of humour and a slight streak of insanity!